Depression
and
Relapse

Depression and Relapse

A Guide to Recovery

By Terence T. Gorski

Based on the Gorski-CENAPS® Model

Additional copies are available from the publisher:
    Herald House/Independence Press
    1001 West Walnut
    P.O. Box 390
    Independence, MO 64051-0390
    Phone: 1-800-767-8181 or (816) 521-3015
    Fax: (816) 521-3066
    Web site: *www.relapse.org*

© 2006 Terence T. Gorski

11 10 09 08 07 06   5 4 3 2 1

CENAPS®
6147 Deltona Blvd.
Spring Hill, FL 34606
Phone: (352) 596-8000
Fax: (352) 596-8002
E-mail: *info@cenaps.com*

ISBN 10: 0-8309-1213-4
ISBN 13: 978-0-8309-1213-1
Printed in the United States of America
Printed and distributed by Herald House/Independence Press

Table of Contents

5

Introduction

Over the years I've seen many recovering people battle with the demons of depression. Some did so successfully. They were able to manage their depression, stay sober, and emerge from each episode of depression with improved recovery skills. Unfortunately, I've seen other people who were not so lucky. They became depressed in recovery, and their depression was severe and prolonged. Nothing seemed to help. They talked about their depression at Twelve-Step meetings and were told things like "This too shall pass." They worked the steps and found they either didn't help or made their depression worse. They tried to find treatment for both addiction and depression, but couldn't. They either ended up in addiction programs that ignored the depression or mental health programs that tended to ignore or misunderstand their addiction. As a result, they couldn't find the help or support they needed to manage their depression and stay in recovery from addiction. Many of them relapsed. Some even attempted suicide or actually killed themselves in sobriety.

My commitment to relapse prevention originally began as a result of one of these unfortunate recovering people. I'll call him John W. John was in his tenth year of sobriety when he was diagnosed with lung cancer. He started chemotherapy and shortly after that started getting depressed. His normal positive attitude turned negative, his bright mood became dark and bleak. He lost energy and motivation. He felt his life wasn't worth living. Everything was an effort. He told people that it felt like he would never feel good again.

Everyone just assumed John would handle it. After all, John was a survivor. He quit drinking and overcame addiction to both heroin and cocaine. He was sober for ten years and was a leader in Twelve-Step programs in his community. He had helped literally hundreds of people find sobriety around the tables of Alcoholics Anonymous (AA), Narcotics Anonymous (NA), and Cocaine Anonymous (CA). We all knew that John was feeling bad, but we thought that when his chemotherapy ended he'd go back to his old self. There was only one problem: John W. committed suicide by taking an overdose of pain pills before his chemotherapy was over.

Everyone was shocked. I wondered why no one, including myself, took his depression seriously. We just assumed his doctor, his Twelve-Step program, and his family and friends would be enough to see him through. No one ever thought he would start feeling so hopeless that he would commit suicide. As we looked back, it was obvious that he was depressed and suicidal. But none of us noticed. I guess we didn't know enough about depression and suicide. Those of us who did know didn't want to believe that someone like John could be brought down by depression.

As a result of his death, I began thinking about the people I knew who had relapsed. I realized that many of them had been depressed. I also realized that most had not received any specialized treatment for their depression. That led me to study the problem more thoroughly. This book is my attempt to share with you what I've learned.

I've worked in the field of addiction and mental health services for more than thirty-five years. I've specialized in treating addicted people and their families. I was especially drawn to chronically relapse-prone people. *Relapse-prone people* recognize that they're addicted, make sincere attempts to stop using alcohol and other drugs, use recovery tools like professional treatment and self-help programs, but return to alcohol and drug use despite their commitment to stay sober.

In working with these chronically relapse-prone people, I discovered three things: First, no one is immune to the disease of addiction. Second, few people are immune to depression. Third, when addiction and depression coexist, the risk of relapse goes way up.

This book is titled *Depression and Relapse: A Guide to Recovery.* I'll explain what addiction is and how untreated depression can contribute to relapse in people recovering from addiction. I'll also show how treating addicted people for depression without specifically treating the addiction can also contribute to relapse. This book will explore the relationship among four things: addiction, depression, recovery, and relapse.

This book will explore the relationship among four things: addiction, depression, recovery, and relapse.

Part 1: Addiction. Part 1 will describe addiction as a biopsychosocial illness. I will use a biopsychosocial model to show you how the symptoms of addiction and the symptoms of depression can interact and reinforce each other. I will put a special emphasis on understanding how depression can lead to addiction relapse and how addiction relapse can activate or reactivate the symptoms of depression.

Part 2: Depression. Part 2 will describe depression and give you the information you'll need to recognize depression in yourself and those you know and love. I'll address depression from a biopsychosocial perspective. In other words, I'll describe the biological (bio), psychological (psycho), and social symptoms of depression. I'll show you how the biological, psychological, and social symptoms work together to form a powerful trap that can turn a single episode of depressive illness into a long-term sequence of symptoms that becomes a chronic nightmare of hopelessness, helplessness, and despair.

Part 3: Recovery. Part 3 will describe the process of recovery for people who are suffering from the co-occurring problems of addiction and depression. Special emphasis will be placed on the specific things that recovering persons and their families and friends can do to manage depression while maintaining sobriety and a strong addiction focus in recovery.

Part 4: Relapse. Part 4 will describe the problem of relapse and discuss how depression can become a complicating factor to addiction recovery. In this part of the book I'll explore the general process of relapse and show how people who have co-occurring depressive illness will tend to experience unique depression-related relapse warning signs that can lead them back to using alcohol and other drugs (AODs).

I'm writing this book for a variety of people. My goal is to help recovering people and their friends and family gain a better understanding of addiction and what they can do in recovery to successfully manage depression without relapsing to addiction. My goal is also to help addiction and mental health professionals gain a better understanding of how addiction and depression interact with each other and what can be done to address these two serious problems in treatment.

Part 1: Addiction

In this part of the book we're going to look at the problems people have with alcohol and other drugs. Alcohol and drug problems are common. About two-thirds of all Americans drink; about one-third don't. Of those who drink, about half develop alcohol-related problems. Somewhere between 6 and 10 percent of all Americans will become alcoholics. In addition to alcohol, many people use, abuse, and become addicted to both prescription and illegal drugs. When you add it all together, about 15 percent of all people will have serious problems with alcohol or other drugs at some point in their lives.

One thing is certain—no one starts drinking or drugging with the goal of getting addicted. People don't wake up in the morning and say, "Gee, this is a beautiful day. I think I'll go out and get addicted!" That just isn't how it works. Addiction is a slow, insidious process. It sneaks up on people from behind, when they're not looking. Here's how it happens.

When some people start using alcohol and other drugs they feel really good. The drugs make them feel better than they've ever felt before, and so they keep drinking and drugging. They focus on enjoying the good times and get in the habit of pushing the bad times out of their minds. This allows the disease of addiction to quietly sneak in through the back door. *The Big Book of Alcoholics Anonymous* states it better than I ever could when it says that addiction is "cunning, baffling, and powerful." Addiction comes into our lives posing as a friend and then slowly grows into a monster that destroys us.

There was once a man named Ted. His best friend gave him a little kitten. Ted loved that soft, cuddly little cat and made it a part of his life. As time went by the cat kept growing. It started to get so big that it was causing problems. It would knock things off the counters, break things, and tear up the house. But Ted loved the cat so much that he decided to ignore the problems. By the time the cat was six months old, it was clear to everyone that this was no ordinary cat. Ted's friend had given him a baby mountain lion. But knowing this didn't change Ted's mind. He loved his "cat" so much that he decided to keep it. After all, what harm could it do? About eight months later a friend came over to visit. Ted's mountain lion attacked his friend. When Ted tried to pull the cat off of his friend, the mountain lion turned on its master. Ted was severely clawed and nearly died.

Addiction is a lot like Ted's mountain lion. It starts out as a cute and cuddly little thing that brings a lot of joy, fun, and excitement into our lives. But then the addiction starts to grow up. As it grows, it turns into a vicious monster that starts destroying our lives.

To understand the relationship between depression and substance-use problems we need to understand three basic things: social and recreational use, substance abuse, and addiction.

1-1. Social and Recreational Use

Social drinking is the responsible use of alcohol to enhance pleasant social interactions. A recent government report (Dufour, 1999) described what social drinking looks like. A social drinker uses alcohol less than three times per week and consumes two normal-sized drinks or less during each drinking episodes. A normal-sized drink equals 12 ounces of regular beer, 5 ounces of wine, or 1.5 ounces of 80-proof distilled spirits such as bourbon, gin, or vodka. Social drinkers become intoxicated less than once a year. When they do get intoxicated, it is usually a planned event such as a New Years Eve party, a wedding, or some other celebration.

Social drinkers never engage in dangerous behavior such as driving a car, operating dangerous equipment, or caring for infants or children while drinking. They never have problems as a result of drinking.

There is no such thing as the social or recreational use of illegal or prescription drugs. This may sound like an extreme statement, but it's true. Whenever people use an illegal drug they're breaking the law. The minute they break the law by using the illegal drug they become a substance abuser. Why is this? Well, people become substance abusers when they start having problems as a result of using alcohol or other drugs. Breaking the law is a problem. By breaking the drug laws people put themselves at risk of getting arrested and going to jail. By any rational definition, when people do things that could put them in jail, it's a problem.

It's a good idea to think twice about using illegal drugs for a number of reasons. *First*, as we said, they're illegal. If you're caught using them you can go to jail. *Second,* they're dangerous. When you buy street drugs you never know what you're getting. The drugs could contain adulterants that are poisonous. *Third,* you don't know the purity or potency. This puts you at high risk of taking an unintentional overdose. *Fourth,* to buy drugs you have to get involved in a violent and antisocial drug culture. Drug dealers are not nice people. They routinely cheat, steal, hurt, and kill people. *Fifth*, you put yourself outside the protection of the law. Short of carrying a gun and being willing to use it, there are very few ways of protecting yourself from the violence of the drug trade. So, there's no such thing as the recreational use of **illegal drugs**.

There's also no such thing as the recreational use of **prescription drugs**. Any time you manipulate a doctor into giving you a prescription that you don't really need you instantly become a substance abuser. Why? Once again, you're breaking the law. You're manipulating the doctor to give you a legally controlled substance by providing false information. This is both dishonest and illegal. You're abusing prescription drugs if you start using more medication than your doctor prescribed. You're also abusing prescription drugs if you start using them to get high instead of to treat an illness.

Evan was an eighteen-year-old high school senior with a promising future in basketball. Coming home from his after-school job at a convenience store, he was pulled over by the police. Being young and cocky, he antagonized the police officer, who decided to search his car. The officer found a minimum quantity of cocaine and marijuana and arrested Evan. The judge decided to impose treatment instead of a sentence, and Evan dutifully completed his three-month outpatient treatment. A few months later, over the Christmas holidays, Evan decided to party with friends and took what he thought was methadone. Evan spent the next two weeks in intensive care where he died from the complications of the overdose. The methadone Evan took was laced with acetaminophen which significantly raised Evans body temperature and essentially cooked his brain.

Here's another point that many people never think about: responsible people will use only their own prescriptions. They'll never share their prescription medication with others. They'll also never use drugs that were prescribed for others. No matter how much you'd like to believe that using illegal or prescribed drugs to get high is "recreational drug use," it's not.

1-2. Substance Abuse

Substance Abusers are people who get into trouble because they make bad decisions about their drinking and drugging. How can you tell if you're a substance abuser? It's easy. If you get into trouble as a result of using alcohol or other drugs you're a substance abuser. It's just that simple. There's a formula that clarifies this definition:

Alcohol and Drug Use + Problems = Substance Abuse

What kind of problems can substance abusers develop as a result of using alcohol or other drugs? Some people develop *physical health problems*. They get physically sick. Others develop *psychological prob-*

lems. They start feeling bad, guilty, or ashamed of their drinking and drugging or of what they do while they're drinking or drugging.

Many start to get **psychologically dysfunctional**. They can't think clearly. They have trouble managing their feelings and emotions. They lose control of their behavior and start doing things they normally wouldn't do. They emotionally overreact and lose their temper. Sometimes they become violent by getting into fights.

Some people develop **social problems**. They neglect important family or social responsibilities. They start having problems at work, with friends, or with their families. Some abusers have financial problems because they spend too much money on drinking or drugging. Others start having legal problems, like getting arrested for drunk driving or for the possession of illegal drugs.

Alcohol and drug abusers have problems as a result of their alcohol and drug use, but they haven't lost control. They haven't yet developed the biological brain responses that create the powerful compulsion to use. They still have the ability to stop.

1-3. Addiction

Addiction is a biopsychosocial illness or disease. The term biopsychosocial is a big word that can be broken down into three parts. The first part of the word is *"bio"*—which stands for biological or pertaining to the body. The second part of the word is *"psycho"* meaning psychological or pertaining to the mind. The third part of the word is *"social"* or pertaining to relationships with people.

Bio – Psycho – Social
BIO = Biological (of the body) PSYCHO = Psychological (thoughts, feelings, behavior) SOCIAL = Relationships and Culture

Substance abusers cross the line into addiction when they start having addictive brain responses that cause neurotransmitter imbalances and start causing progressive brain dysfunction.

Addiction is a *primary disease or disorder* that results in the abuse of, dependence upon, and addiction to mind-altering chemicals. Addiction causes alcohol- and drug-induced brain dysfunction that disorganizes the personality and causes social and occupational problems.

On a *biological level*, addiction causes *brain dysfunction*. People with a *genetic history of addiction* are more susceptible to alcohol and drug-related brain dysfunction. This means that if other members of your family have had serious alcohol or drug problems, you may have inherited the genetic tendency to develop the same problems.

On a *psychological level*, the progressive brain dysfunction starts causing problems with thinking, managing feelings, and controlling behavior. The progressive brain dysfunction also starts causing problems with managing stress, remembering things, and sleeping restfully.

The most disruptive psychological symptom is *loss of control*. When addicted people start using alcohol and other drugs, they never know what is going to happen. Any time they start using alcohol or other drugs, a brain chemistry response can be activated that impairs judgment and impulse control. This brain chemistry response can cause them to lose control and start doing things that they normally wouldn't do.

As these problems keep getting worse, the addiction causes *personality disorganization* that damages the addict's identity. Some of this personality disorganization is temporary and will spontaneously go away with abstinence as the brain recovers from the dysfunction. Other personality traits will become deeply habituated during the addiction. These personality traits will require treatment in order to subside.

On a **social level**, the personality disorganization causes progressive social dysfunction. Addicts start having progressive problems at home, at work, and with their friends.

1-4. Addiction as a Brain Disease

Addiction is a brain disease. Whenever addicted people use alcohol or other drugs their brains go through a progression of three abnormal brain chemistry reactions. These abnormal reactions make it easy for them to keep drinking and drugging while making it difficult for them to stop and stay stopped.

Addictive Brain Chemistry Responses make people want to keep using alcohol and drugs.

Neurotransmitter Imbalances make it difficult for people to stop and stay stopped.

Substance-Induced Brain Dysfunction makes it difficult for people to recognize their addiction and start a recovery program.

Not all substance abusers have all three of these brain chemistry problems. Most, however, have at least one. Let's look at each one of these abnormal brain responses in a little more detail.

Addictive Brain Chemistry Responses

The *Addictive Brain Chemistry Response* does two things: it floods the brain with pleasure chemicals, and then it deprives the brain of warning chemicals.

Addictive Brain Chemistry Response

1. Floods the brain with pleasure chemicals
2. Deprives the brain of warning chemicals

The flood of pleasure chemicals makes people feel really good by normalizing their brain chemistry and creating an intense feeling of euphoria.

The deprivation of warning chemicals block out the feeling of danger or threat. These warning chemicals normally flood the brain whenever we're in danger or facing a serious threat.

The job of these warning chemicals is to make us feel so uncomfortable that we start looking around to see what's wrong. When the Addictive Brain Chemistry Response slows down or stops the production of these warning chemicals, nothing feels threatening. Nothing scares us or makes us feel concerned. It seems like nothing can hurt us. As a result, good judgment goes out the window and people can start doing dangerous things without even realizing it.

It was July 4th and Hank and his friends had had too much to drink, so going out and screaming through the neighborhood on their motorcycles seemed like a good idea. The officer who responded to the breaking-the-peace dispatch could not establish control and called for backup. The motorcyclists taunted and cursed at the officers and began to tear up many of the neighborhood yards. The officers tried everything they could think of and so, right or wrong, they decided to physically confront the men with their patrol cars. They parked in a driveway and ran over Hank as he came speeding down the street. Hank spent the next nine months in a body cast and lived with a steel rod in his leg for thirty years. Although the evening went seriously wrong, Hank's drinking impaired his judgment which resulted in some very bad consequences.

When high-risk people stop using alcohol and other drugs, the brain doesn't just go back to normal. There is a **rebound in brain chemistry** that causes the levels of pleasure chemicals in the brain to go up and down in a chaotic and unpredictable way. The brain stops producing the pleasure chemicals that are flooding the brain. This causes the level of pleasure chemicals to drop rapidly. They often drop so fast that they go below the normal level before the brain turns production back on.

The brain also turns on the production of the *warning chemicals*. This causes the level of warning chemicals to rapidly increase. The warning chemicals often rise above normal levels before the brain slows down production. This creates a feeling of threat and anxiety. As a result there is a period where the brain chemistry is unstable and fluctuating. The brain swings from not having enough pleasure chemicals to feel good to having a flood of pleasure chemicals that makes them feel euphoric. At the same time, the brain swings from having so many warning chemicals that make them feel paranoid and hypervigilant to having too few warning chemicals that make them feel an unrealistic sense of courage and confidence.

This process keeps reversing itself. The pleasure chemicals spike back up. The warning chemicals drop back down. The chemistry of the brain vibrates like a guitar string as the levels of brain chemicals shift back and forth from too high to too low until the brain eventually gets back into a normal balance. These fluctuations in brain chemistry make people feel agitated and depressed. It makes it hard to think clearly. They have trouble solving usually simple problems. Emotionally they either start overreacting or they become emotionally numb and can't tell what they're feeling. They also have trouble controlling their behavior and can do things that they normally wouldn't do. They can't remember things and have a tough time sleeping restfully. And as high-risk people use more alcohol and drugs over a longer period of time the symptoms keep getting worse and lasting longer.

Neurotransmitter Imbalances

The good feelings caused by alcohol and drug use make it hard to believe that the substances are damaging your brain. But they are!

While the flood of pleasure chemicals and the deprivation of warning chemicals are making high-risk people feel euphoric, the drugs are damaging the brain by creating serious *Neurotransmitter Imbalances*.

Neurotransmitter Imbalances are deficiencies and excesses in neurotransmitter levels which can produce profound disruptions in physical and behavioral

25

processes. Some of the possible effects of neurotransmitter imbalances are

- Sleep disturbances
- Anxiety
- Depression
- Inability to think or concentrate
- Impulsivity
- Aggression
- Suicidal behavior
- Violence
- Psychosis
- Schizophrenia

This is not an exhaustive list of possible effects for the surge or depletion of various neurotransmitters. Furthermore, the swing in neurotransmitter levels produces adverse effects on the heart, circulatory system, respiration, body temperature, and other physical processes.

These imbalances can cause high-risk people to be in a constant state of agitated depression.

Some high-risk people develop these imbalances as a result of heavy and abusive drinking and drugging. Other people seem to be born with them. They struggle with agitated depression all of their lives. When they first use their drug of choice, they experience a powerful sense of release. They feel normal for the first time.

No matter what causes these neurotransmitter imbalances, there's one sure thing: the continued use of alcohol and other drugs will causes them to get worse. As the neurotransmitter imbalances get worse, the agitated depression that occurs between alcohol and drug use episodes will also get worse. This agitated depression makes day-to-day living a continuous struggle. And so people feel miserable whenever they're not drinking and drugging. They become desperate. They want to find something, anything that will make them feel better.

Substance-Induced Brain Dysfunction

The brains of high-risk people are more easily damaged by alcohol and other drugs than the brains of low risk people.

High-risk people tend to experience more brain dysfunction, even if they use the same amount, at the same frequency, for the same period of time. It also takes longer for the brains of high-risk people to recover from the effects of an episode of drinking and drug use. The brain of a low-risk person who gets drunk on Saturday night will fully recover by Monday morning. The brain of a high-risk person will show signs of neuropsychological impairment seven to ten days later. This is because the physical predisposition to addiction makes the brain more vulnerable to damage and less able to quickly recover from the effects of alcohol and drug use.

As a result, most addicted people eventually develop *Substance-Induced Brain Dysfunction*. These symptoms of brain dysfunction cause problems when people stop using. When they stop, they can't think clearly and can get easily confused. They feel emotionally numb and then suddenly overreact for no apparent reason. These emotional overreactions make it difficult for them to control their behavior.

Because this is all happening when they're not using, they don't think it has anything to do with their drinking and drugging. When they start drinking or drugging again, the addictive brain responses make these problems temporarily disappear.

1-5. The Progression from Abuse to Addiction

It's important to notice that there is often a progression from substance use, to substance abuse, to substance addiction. Here's how it works.

Progression to Addiction

1. Non-Problem Use
2. Frequent and Heavy Use
3. Abuse (Use that Causes Problems)
4. Addiction (Brain Chemistry Changes from Frequent and Heavy Use)

Non-Problem Use

People start using alcohol and drugs in a casual and infrequent way that doesn't cause problems. Let's call this *Non-Problem Use*.

Frequent and Heavy Use

As people experience the positive effects from using alcohol and drugs, they start using more frequently and heavily. They're still not having any problems, but they're starting to use so much that other people are noticing.

Research suggests that anyone who has more than three normal-sized drinks more than twice per week is at high risk of developing alcoholism. Most alcoholic people drink significantly more than this. When they say they would like to be social drinkers, what they actually mean is that they would like to drink as much alcohol as they like, as often as they like, while getting the mood-altering effect they want, without experiencing any pain or problems. Most alcoholics would be unwilling to even try to drink two drinks twice per week or less. When I suggested this to one alcoholic I was working with, his response was, "What would be the point? That's not even drinking!"

Abuse (Use that Causes Problems)

As the quantity and frequency of alcohol and drug use increases, people slowly start to have problems. They gradually move into a pattern of abuse. Remember, abuse is using alcohol and other drugs in a way that causes problems. Typically these problems begin in the family and then spread to close friends. By the time employment is affected, family and friendships have usually been seriously damaged by the substance abuse.

At the age of twenty-three, Clay had lost his driver's license for life and bought a new identity. He was a recreational cocaine user and sold a little on the side to pay for his drugs. Because his source was in North Philadelphia, he knew it was prudent to carry a small gun. One evening a friend called and said he had some friends in town and could Clay fix them up. The friend couldn't get away but wanted to send someone over to buy. Clay obliged an old friend and met him in the driveway. No sooner did he accept the cash than a swarm of DEA agents were all over him. Clay was sentenced to fifteen years in prison for possession, sale, and concealed weapons charges. His recreational drug use clearly had him by the tail feathers.

Addiction

Substance abusers continue to use frequently and heavily until the alcohol and other drugs start causing changes in brain chemistry. These changes in brain chemistry activate the disease of addiction. Once the addiction is activated there's no turning back. The addiction takes on a life of its own and will continue to progress as long as the person keeps using alcohol and other drugs.

1-6. The Stages of Addiction

Addiction is a biopsychosocial disease that progresses through three predictable stages.

Stages of Addiction

1. **Early Stage (Growing Dependency)**
2. **Middle Stage (Progressive Loss of Control)**
3. **Late Stage (Deterioration)**

Early-Stage Addiction (Growing Dependency)

First, there's an early stage of addiction marked by a *growing dependency* on alcohol and other drugs.

During this stage, the alcohol and drugs are still making people feel good. They're still allowing people to function well. There are no serious problems so the early stage addict keeps on drinking and drugging. As tolerance develops they gradually start using more and more.

Middle-Stage Addiction (Progressive Loss of Control)

As people continue to use more and more, they move into the middle stages of addiction. The middle stages are marked by *progressive loss of control* over the use of alcohol and other drugs.

Sometimes when the middle-stage addict starts drinking and drugging, everything goes well. They get the effect they want from drinking and drugging. They use in moderation. They don't get into trouble or do anything they're ashamed or embarrassed about later. At other times, however, they lose control. They use more alcohol or drugs than they intended to use. Their judgment goes out the window and they use for longer periods of time than they planned. Sometimes they miss important events because they lose track of time. They do things while drinking and drugging that they never intended to do. As a result, they start feeling guilty and ashamed. As the alcohol and drug-related problems become more severe, they start to get scared. But there are still some good times drinking and drugging, so they rationalize the problems away and start making solemn commitments to themselves to clean up their act. "I'll never get that drunk or stoned again," they promise themselves. The problem is they never define exactly how much is "that much." So when it happens again, they can rationalize the problem away again. Then they can forget about it—and then forget that they forgot. This creates the illusion that the problem never happened. In reality, however, the problems are happening—and they're getting worse. Reality doesn't go away just because you pretend it doesn't exist.

Late-Stage Addiction (Deterioration)

Then people start moving into the late stages of addiction. The late stages are marked by *progressive physical, psychological, and social deterioration.*

31

Late-stage addicts start getting sick. They start having alcohol and drug-related health problems and those problems keep getting worse. Psychologically, they start falling apart. They feel ashamed and guilty about what's happening to them as a result of their alcohol and drug use, so they push other people away and start isolating. If their friends get concerned, they brush them off, tell them some convenient lies, and give the clear message to mind their own business. They try to stop drinking and drugging but they can't stay stopped.

This starts destroying their confidence and self-esteem. They start getting scared and usually go underground. They try to hide their alcohol and drug use. But by this time they're having serious social problems that are starting to catch up with them. Their families and friends are worried and angry. They're having serious problems on the job. The cost of maintaining their addiction is causing serious financial problems. They're also having legal problems—nothing serious, just "little problems" like getting caught drinking or drugging on the job, getting arrested for driving under the influence of alcohol, or possessing and using illegal drugs.

The problems keep getting worse until one of four things happens: they die as a result of an alcohol- or drug-related illness or accident; they commit suicide to end the pain; they are put in jail or a mental institution; or they go into treatment for their addiction.

These are the only four possible long-term outcomes of progressive addiction. I want to repeat them one more time. If you have this disease, I want to be sure you know exactly where it's taking you.

If you keep drinking and drugging, you'll die from an alcohol or drug related illness or accident; you'll commit suicide to end the pain; you'll get put in jail or a mental institution; or you'll recognize that you're addicted, get treatment, and make a commitment to work a personal recovery program. That's it! There are no other choices.

1-7. Progressive Symptoms of Addiction

Addiction has a number of progressive symptoms. I want to review this symptom progression so you can learn how to recognize these symptoms in yourself and other people.

1. Chronic Low-Grade Agitated Depression:

Due to the abnormally low release of brain-reward chemicals, the person experiences a chronic state of low-grade agitated depression. This state is dysphoric and creates a strong need for relief and the urge to find something, anything, that will relieve this state.

2. Biological Reinforcement:

As a result of normal social pressure, the person experiments with alcohol and other drugs. They find a drug of choice that activates the release of brain-reward chemicals. The result is an intense feeling of euphoria and personal well-being. For the first time, the person's mood normalizes and they feel good. They can experience pleasure. Whatever feelings they are experiencing before use become normalized. As a result, the drug of choice can be used as a psychoactive medication.

3. Euphoric Recall:

The biological reinforcement creates a positive experience. The person uses their sensory memory to construct detailed memories of how this state of euphoria felt. They then use a process of *euphoric recall* by exaggerating the memory of how good the experience felt. They also block out or minimize any negative aspects of the memory. This sensory memory of the euphoric experience stimulates the limbic system to develop an emotional urge to repeat the experience. This emotional urge, as it grows strong, can activate a primitive tissue hunger for the drug which is called craving.

4. Positive Expectancy:

The person begins to create idealized fantasies about how good it will feel to use the drug of choice. They begin to imagine the details of how they believe this state of euphoria will feel. The strong expectancy and anticipation of the strong mood-altering effect reinforces the craving and motivates the person to begin seeking out the drug of choice.

Craving is the overwhelming and intense desire for the drug of choice. It refers to the hunger for alcohol before drinking begins.

5. Awfulizing Abstinence:

The person notices how uncomfortable it is when not using the drug of choice. They also notice how little pleasure they are able to experience when not using their drug of choice. They begin using a psychological process called *awfulizing abstinence* in which they exaggerate how bad it feels to be without their drug of choice and block or minimize any positive experience they may have when not using their drug of choice. As a result, they develop a negative expectancy of what abstinence from the drug of choice will be like.

6. Regular Use:

The person begins to use the drug of choice on a regular and frequent basis in order to experience the euphoric effect and to avoid the discomfort of being without their drug of choice.

7. High Tolerance:

It takes more and more of the drug of choice to create the desired feeling of euphoria. The person also develops the ability to use progressively larger amounts of the drug of choice without becoming intoxicated or impaired. As a result, they can use frequently and heavily without apparent adverse consequences.

8. Hangover Resistance:

The person experiences minimal sickness on the morning after using alcohol and drugs. This rapid recovery allows the person to use the drug of choice frequently. It also creates the illusion that it is safe to use the drug of choice and that there are no adverse consequences.

9. Addictive Beliefs:

As a result of the experiences created by the biological reinforcement, high tolerance, and hangover resistance, the person comes to believe that the drug of choice is good for them and will magically fix them or make them better. They also believe that not using their drug of choice is bad for them. They come to view people who support their alcohol and drug use as friends and people who fail to support it as their enemies.

10. Obsession and Compulsion:

The person begins spending a large amount of time thinking about how good it is to use their drug of choice and how bad they feel when not using it. These thoughts become obsessive and begin to intrude into moments when it would be better to be thinking about other things. Obsession is a thought disorder that affects the cerebral cortex. The obsessive thoughts create a compulsion or strong urge to use the drug of choice. The compulsion is an affective disorder that affects the limbic system. Eventually brain chemistry is altered and the obsession and compulsion escalates into a craving. Craving is a primitive drive disorder that affects the primitive drive centers of the brain stem.

11. A Pattern of Heavy and Regular Use:

The person begins to use their drug of choice regularly and heavily. They develop a deeply habituated pattern of *drug-seeking behavior* as a result of the routine rituals involved in preparing to use their drug of choice, using it, and recovering from its use.

12. Addictive Lifestyle:

The person attracts and is attracted to other individuals who share strong positive attitudes toward the use of alcohol and other drugs. They begin to construct the routines of their lifestyle around people, places, and things that support their use of their drug of choice. As a result, they become immersed in an addiction-centered subculture and a social network of people who share strong positive attitudes toward the use of alcohol and other drugs.

13. Addictive Lifestyle Losses:
The person distances people who support sobriety and surround themselves with people who support alcohol and drug use.

14. Loss of Behavioral Control:
The person also begins to use larger amounts with greater frequency. They start having growing problems with judgment, impulse control, problem solving, and rigid repetitive thinking. They begin to experience progressive physical, psychological, and social problems.

15. Denial:
The person is unable to recognize the pattern of problems related to the use of alcohol and drugs. They begin to use unconscious denial mechanisms to protect themselves from experiencing the pain of facing the progressive pattern of severe problems. They avoid thinking and talking about their alcohol and drug use. When questioned about it they absolutely deny that they are worried or that there are any problems. When confronted with alcohol and drug-related problems they minimize how serious they are and convince themselves that the problems are being blown out of proportion. They rationalize by developing good reasons for drinking and drugging and good reasons for having the problems. They also start blaming by developing scape-

goats upon whom they place the responsibility for the problems.

16. Addictive Problems and Lifestyle Losses:

The person begins to experience the loss of important people and lifestyle activities as a result of their total immersion in an addictive lifestyle, the distancing of people and activities that support sobriety, and the progressive pattern of developing problems and life crisis.

17. Progressive Neurological and Neuropsychological Impairments:

The progressive damage of alcohol and drugs to the brain creates growing problems with judgment and impulse control. As a result, behavior begins to spiral out of control. The cognitive capacities needed to think abstractly to solve problems become impaired. The person becomes locked into a repetitive behavior pattern marked by denial and circular reasoning, which progresses to more frequent and heavy substance use.

18. Degeneration:

The person begins to experience physical, psychological and social deterioration. Unless the person develops an unexpected insight or is confronted by problems or people in their life, the progressive problems are likely to continue until serious damage results.

19. Inability to Abstain:

The person attempts to abstain but is plagued by acute withdrawal and the longer-term withdrawal symptoms associated with chronic brain toxicity. In addiction, the low-grade agitated depression and symptoms of anhedonia (the inability to experience pleasure from normally pleasurable experiences) return. The combination of problems impairs judgment and impulse control. When coupled with the addictive belief system and the deeply ingrained pattern of obsession, compulsion, and craving, the person becomes unable to maintain abstinence and relapses.

1-8. Depression and Addiction

Depression is a significant complicating factor in recovery from substance-use disorders. Nearly all substance abusers show significant depression in the first several weeks of recovery. In most cases, the depression quickly subsides. Others, however, suffer from serious bouts of depression throughout their recovery.

Depression is a serious problem for many chemically dependent people that can lead to relapse. In any given year, 10 percent of the population or about 19 million American adults will suffer from depression. At least 12 percent of the adult population will have an episode of depression that is serious enough to warrant treatment at some point in their lives. (NIMH 2002)

Severity of Depression in Recovering People

The severity of depression in people recovering from addiction tends to follow a rule of thirds with about one-third of all recovering people falling into each category. The categories are Mild Short-term Depression, Severe Short-term Depression, and Severe Long-term Depression. Let's take a moment to examine each.

Mild Short-term Depression: In about one-third of recovering people, the symptoms of depression are not severe enough to interfere with recovery and spontaneously diminish with detoxification and life stabilization.

Severe Short-term Depression: In another third of recovering people, the symptoms of depression are so severe during detoxification and stabilization that specialized treatment focusing on the symptoms of depression is needed to keep it from interfering with addiction recovery. The depressive symptoms, however, diminish after detoxification and life stabilization and tend to subside within a period of six to eighteen months. No long-term treatment of depression is required. The depression may recur at a variety of points in recovery, but with proper treatment and renewed commitment to addiction recovery the symptoms subside.

Severe Long-term Depression: Unfortunately, about one-third of all substance-abusing patients will continue to suffer with chronic depression or periodic episodes of severe depression throughout their recovery. For these clients, the depressive symptoms can become a serious problem that leads to relapse. Sometimes this depression is present during detoxification and stabilization of the substance-use disorder. Sometimes the depression develops after stabilization has been completed.

1.9. Patterns of Depression and Addiction

In chemically dependent patients, depression often presents itself in one of four common patterns:

Substance-Induced Depression, Depression-Induced Substance Abuse, Situational Depression in Sobriety, and Co-occurring Addiction and Depression. To avoid relapse it is critical to recognize these four types of depression and to match patients to appropriate treatment strategies.

Chemical Dependence and Depression Common Patterns

1. Substance-Induced Depression
2. Depression-Induced Substance Abuse
3. Situational Depression in Sobriety
4. Co-occurring Addiction and Depression

---

1. Substance-Induced Depression

Substance-Induced Depression is caused by the use, abuse, and addiction to alcohol and other drugs. A depressive episode develops in early abstinence that is related to detoxification, acute withdrawal, or post acute withdrawal (PAW). The symptoms of depression are linked to substance use with no indicators of an independent depressive illness. The depression begins to spontaneously remit as the symptoms of detoxification, acute withdrawal, and post acute withdrawal subside.

2. Depression-Induced Substance Abuse

Depression-Induced Substance Abuse occurs when patients suffering from depressive illness start using alcohol or other drugs to medicate or manage the symptoms of depression. Unfortunately, alcohol and other drugs of abuse generally make the depression worse instead of better. In the absence of accurate diagnosis and effective treatment, many patients rely on substance abuse as their only

41

source of relief because they have no other known alternative. These patients meet the criteria of substance abuse, but the abuse is clearly linked to efforts to manage the depressed mood. There is no evidence of tolerance, withdrawal, or progressive loss of control. Once the depression lifts, the urge to use alcohol and other drugs disappears or radically diminishes without recurrent or persistent urges or craving. Some patients start abusing drugs to manage the symptoms of the depression and then develop a co-occurring substance-use disorder that is independent of the depression. For more details refer to the description of co-occurring addiction and depression on page 43.

Frank was sixty-two years old and a decorated Korean War veteran. He had been using alcohol for years to manage his nightmares and night terrors that he brought back from the war. The drinking was interfering with his job and his family life. His wife of forty years told him he had to get help or she would leave him. He tried again and again to stop drinking, but couldn't do it on his own. He believed he was too old for Alcoholics Anonymous and that nothing would really help. His wife was serious about his stopping or her leaving. When he said he just couldn't stop, she left. A few weeks later she saw an attorney and Frank was served divorce papers. That afternoon he drank a fifth of scotch, put on his military uniform, and spent the rest of the day in the garage with the Jeep running. Frank's death was ruled a suicide by carbon monoxide poisoning. Frank really died from untreated post-traumatic stress disorder, depression, and alcoholism.

3. Situational Depression in Sobriety

Situational Depression in Sobriety occurs in some chemically dependent patients who experience extreme stressors or inadequate treatment in recovery. These patients usually attempt abstinence without identifying or changing addictive patterns of thinking, managing feelings, behaving, and structuring their lifestyle. As a result, there is a gradual buildup of stress and progressive dysfunction in sobriety. As the stress and problems escalate, many patients feel trapped and hopeless and become depressed. The depression, however, is clearly linked to the mismanagement of problems in sobriety. This is often coupled with post acute withdrawal and the absence of proper diet, exercise, and stress management practices necessary to stabilization of brain-chemistry imbalances caused by the addiction.

4. Co-occurring Depressive Illness

Co-occurring Depressive Illness occurs when patients are suffering from both chemical dependency and an independent depressive illness. These patients typically have a family history of substance abuse and addiction, and a family history of depression or other mood disorders. The history reveals that the symptoms of the depression predated the chemical abuse and that as the addiction progressed so did the severity of the depression. There is often a vacillating symptom pattern. The depression temporarily goes into remission when the patient is drinking or drugging only to return in a severe form when the patient attempts abstinence. With co-occurring depressive illness, both the chemical dependence and the depression need to be treated simultaneously.

Remember the story of Frank, who suffered from untreated PTSD, depression, and alcoholism? Frank had a family history of depression which was not known until after his suicide, but may speak volumes to the children he left behind. Frank had a grandfather, Ted, who also drank heavily. Under eerily similar circumstances, Ted's wife left him because of his drinking. The day Ted was served with divorce papers he killed himself with the gas from the kitchen stove. Two depressed alcoholics who both succeeded with suicide. Frank left a son behind who is also an alcoholic. However, his son is in recovery and regularly attends Alcoholics Anonymous.

1-10. Reciprocal Relapse

Untreated depression can cause a relapse to chemical dependency. Untreated chemical dependency can cause a relapse to depression. As a result, the two disorders must be treated simultaneously. Depression and its related feelings of hopelessness and helplessness can become so severe that it interferes with the ability to maintain a recovery program. The depression can activate addictive thinking that creates a compulsion to use alcohol or other drugs to medicate the depression.

If recovering people do not have an adequate recovery program for chemical dependency, then the problems of coping with addictive thinking and behaviors, managing craving, and changing from an alcohol and drug-centered lifestyle to a sobriety and responsibility-centered lifestyle can become overwhelming and trigger depression. Once the depression is activated, the risk of using alcohol and drugs increases. Once alcohol and drug use is started, the

44

biological effects of the drugs will trigger a reactivation of the symptoms of depression.

With this general understanding of addiction and depression, we can now move to exploring depression as a co-occurring disorder. Whenever depression becomes severe enough to interfere with ongoing addiction recovery, it is serious enough to seek specific help for managing the symptoms of depression. With this in mind, let's take an in-depth look at the problem of depression.

Part 2: Depression— An Overview

In this part of the book I want to accomplish four things:
1. Explain what depression is and how serious it can be;
2. Explain the difference between depressive illness and the normal ups-and-downs of life;
3. Describe the general dynamics of depression and present a comprehensive symptom list; and
4. Show you how to use this symptom list as a tool for self-assessment and self-monitoring of your progress in recovery.

2-1. What Depression Is and How Serious It Can Be

Depression is a serious public health problem that affects more than 19 million adults in the United States each year. Many will be unnecessarily incapacitated for weeks or months, because their illness goes untreated. The total cost of depression to the nation in 1990 was estimated to be between $30 and

$44 billion. The suffering of depressed people and their families is immeasurable.

People in recovery from addiction are at special risk of developing depressive illness and so are their families. Untreated depression is a common cause of relapse among addicted people. Depression is also a frequently present problem of people living in a family system with an addicted person.

In any serious discussion of depression, it is important to accurately describe terms. In common usage, the term "depression" is often used to describe the bad feelings we all have that result from the normal ups-and-downs of everyday life. These negative or depressed moods are very different from *Major Depression* or *Depressive Disorder*, which is a serious biopsychosocial illness. I'll explain that difference in a few moments. For now, it's important to understand that, whenever I use the term depression, I will be referring to the symptoms of depressive illness.

During any given year, 15 percent of all adults between eighteen and seventy-five years of age will suffer from significant symptoms of depression. Depression accounts for 75 percent of all psychiatric hospitalizations and costs the nation billions of dollars annually. The suicide rate, which is generally regarded as an effective index of the prevalence of depression, has been increasing over the past few years.

2-2. Depression vs. the Normal Ups-and-Downs of Life

Depression (depressive disorders or depressive illness) is a serious medical condition that affects people biologically, psychologically, and socially. Biologically, depression causes serious changes in brain chemistry. These changes affect the part of the brain that regulates mood and emotion. The primary neurotransmitter involved in depression is *serotonin*. When a person becomes depressed, the amount of serotonin available to the brain goes down. The reduced serotonin levels affect the regulation of mood and emotion and set the stage for people to experience depression.

There are differences between depressed moods that are part of normal living and severe states of depression that are part of a depressive illness. Unfortunately, there is no clear black-and-white dividing line that separates the two.

2-3. Types of Depression

There are different types of depressive disorders. These include: major depression, dysthymia (a long-term, milder form of depression), and bipolar disorder (in which episodes of depression cycle to episodes of mania). Within each type there are variations in the number of symptoms, their severity, and persistence.

Major depression is manifested by a combination of symptoms (see the symptom list on page 58) that interfere with the ability to work, study, sleep, eat, and enjoy pleasurable activities. Such a disabling episode of depression may occur only once but more commonly occurs several times in a lifetime.

A less-severe type of depression, *dysthymia*, involves long-term, chronic symptoms that do not disable but keep one from functioning well or from feeling good. Many people with dysthymia also experience major depressive episodes at some time in their lives.

Another type of depression is *bipolar disorder*, also called manic-depressive illness. Not nearly as prevalent as other forms of depressive disorders, bipolar disorder is characterized by cycling mood changes: severe highs (mania) and lows (depression). Sometimes the mood swings are dramatic and rapid, but most often they are gradual. When in the depressed cycle, an individual can have any or all of the symptoms of a depressive disorder. When in the manic cycle, the individual may be overactive, over-talkative, and have a great deal of energy. Mania often affects thinking, judgment, and social behavior in ways that cause serious problems and embarrassment. For example, the individual in a manic phase may feel elated, full of grand schemes that might range from unwise business decisions to romantic sprees. Mania, left untreated, may worsen to a psychotic state.

Here's an example. June, a sixty-seven-year-old woman, recounted her trip to Washington D.C. while in a manic state. She ordered 100 long-stem white roses and meticulously wrote on the stem of each rose the name of a senator and a plea to overturn Roe v. Wade. She was blocked from personally delivering each rose and became belligerent when the Senate guards did not believe that God had personally directed her to "Go forth and have the Senate sin no more." June was hospitalized and treated with medication and cognitive therapy. She appears to be doing well today.

2-4. Continuum of Depression

Depression is a state of central nervous system inhibition that operates on a continuum between severe depression (severe central nervous system inhibition) and severe mania (severe central nervous system stimulation). When a depressed mood becomes so severe that it interferes with normal acts of daily living (normal daily routines necessary to maintain interpersonal relationships, work activities, or the maintenance tasks of life) it is called *depression*. When a stimulated mood becomes so severe that it interferes with normal acts of daily living, it is called *mania*. When a person swings between severely depressed moods and extremely stimulated moods, it is called *manic depression*. This manic-depressive continuum becomes a vital tool in recognizing normal mood swings and distinguishing them from mood disorders. (See diagram below.)

2-5. Normal Mood States Related to Depression

It is normal and natural for healthy people to swing between mild and moderate states of stimulation and depression. We have good days and bad, we feel high and low. Using the depression-mania scale below as a reference point, it's normal for people to swing between a plus three and a minus three in response to the normal ups-and-downs of daily living. It is also common for people to experience an extreme mood state in response to severe psychosocial stressors such as the loss of a loved one, the loss of a job, serious financial setbacks, or other extreme life changes.

Manic-Depressive Continuum

Depressed Mood -10 .....-5 ..... 0 ..... +5 ..... +10 Stimulated Mood

(Depression) ←---→(Mania)

Normally, however, there are *protective factors* that prevent us from getting locked or trapped in extremely depressed or agitated states for prolonged periods of time. These protective factors also keep us from rapidly cycling between agitation and depression. Unfortunately, there are also risk factors that make us more likely to suffer from episodes of depression.

2-6. Risk and Protective Factors

It's helpful to think in terms of protective factors and risk factors. Protective factors are ways of thinking, feeling, acting, and living that protect us from depression. Once these protective skills have become habitual, we find that it takes more stress and pressure to trigger our depression and the episodes of depression become shorter and less severe.

Protective factors are ways of thinking, feeling, acting, and living our lives that protect us from depression.

Risk factors are ways of thinking, feeling, acting, and living our lives that make us more vulnerable to depression. If these risk factors have become a habitual part of our life, we find that it takes much less stress and pressure to trigger our depression and that the episodes of depression become longer and more severe.

Risk factors are ways of thinking, feeling, acting, and living our lives that make us more vulnerable to depression.

The good news is that we can learn to identify these risk and protective factors and make choices to learn and practice protective skills while eliminating or minimizing the use of risk factors.

Let's use Joe, a person with low protective factors and high risk factors, as an example of how this works. Joe comes from a family where his mother, grandmother, and one of his sisters suffered from severe depression (a genetic risk factor). He's learned to be a negative person, always looking for the worst in people and situations (a psychological risk factor). He's socially isolated, has no close friends, and keeps a distance from people at work who call him a loner (social risk factors).

Whenever Joe notices something negative, his brain chemistry reacts by suddenly and dramatically dropping his serotonin level which activates the complex brain chemistry process that underlies depression. Because Joe is isolated and has no one to talk to he begins using *emotional thinking* (If I feel depressed something really bad must be going on so I had better look out). He goes home, isolates himself, clicks on the television and keeps thinking about how helpless, hopeless, and useless his entire life is.

After getting treated for depression, Joe lowered his biological risk of depression by taking antidepressant medications to stabilize his blood chemistry, which raised his serotonin levels. He completed a cognitive therapy group that taught him how to identify and change depressive thinking. He also put together a support network of people. He stopped drinking, started going to Alcoholics Anonymous, and made some good friends who he could call when the depressive thoughts started cycling in his head.

2-7. Depression as a Biopsychosocial Problem

Depression is a biopsychosocial problem. When people become depressed, they are usually experiencing physical, psychological, and social problems that combine to create the severe episode of depression. People who are able to deal with high levels of stress and disappointment without becoming depressed usually have physical, psychological, and social protective factors that allow them to bounce back from adversity. This ability to bounce back from adversity is called *resiliency*. The protective factors that create resiliency operate physically, psychologically, and socially.

On a physical level, our brain chemistry will automatically adjust to different levels of stimulation to bring our mood back into balance. This means that our brain is capable of adapting to high levels of stress and then rebounding from debilitating episodes of stress, pain, and loss. Much of this resiliency is an automatic part of how our brain chemistry adjusts to the stresses and strains of life to allow us to keep responding to life in positive ways.

Unfortunately, some people are born with a tendency to have abnormal physical responses to stress, pain, and loss. Instead of having automatic brain responses that protect them from stress and minimize the likelihood of depression, their brain is easily overwhelmed by stress, pain, and loss and can begin malfunctioning in a way that causes depression.

People with depressive illness have malfunctioning brain systems that are easily overwhelmed by pain, stress, and loss.

On a psychological level, we are capable of noticing extreme moods and making changes in what we think, how we manage our feelings and emotions, and what we do. Some of this is a conscious process. We notice that we are starting to get depressed and consciously identify what we are thinking, feeling, and doing that is contributing to the depression. We can then make choices about changing our thoughts, managing our feelings more effectively, and changing our day-to-day behaviors. As we'll see later, there are proven methods of managing depression that involve these basic psychological changes.

We also have habitual psychological responses to things that happen. These responses occur automatically and unconsciously. We've gotten in the habit of using them so we no longer have to think about it. Some of these automatic thoughts, feelings, and behaviors are depressing. In other words, some of our habitual ways of thinking, feeling, acting, and relating to other people tend to make us depressed. We may be unaware of these automatic habits of thinking, feeling, and acting. So when we get depressed, it seems like the depression is happening for no reason at all.

Unfortunately, this usually isn't true. In observing myself and working with other people suffering from depression I've discovered one important fact: Most people who suffer from depression are habitually using ways of thinking, managing feelings, and behaving that cause them to be depressed or make their depression worse. The good news is that we can learn to identify our depressive ways of thinking, managing feelings, behaving, and living that are making our depression worse and learn how to make changes that will make us feel less depressed.

Mechanisms that Protect Us from Depression

1. **Physical**
   —Brain Chemistry Balance
2. **Psychological**
   —Ways of Thinking, Managing Feelings, and Acting
3. **Social**
   —Honest and Supportive Relationships

We also have social and cultural networks that provide protective relationships. When we get into extreme or destructive moods, people in our social network will begin to point it out to us and encourage us to get back into balance. A big part of dealing with depression is to develop a social support network made up of people who know that we are in recovery from both addiction and depression. We can then talk honestly with these people and receive proper encouragement and support for dealing with difficult moods and emotions.

2-8. Mood Disorders

When a mood disorder is present, people become locked in one of three abnormal emotional states:

1. **Depression:** Extreme sadness, an inhibited state of low energy, and behavioral inertia (the inability to act);
2. **Mania:** High energy that easily escalates in severe agitated and frantic behavior (overstimulation);
3. **Manic-Depression (Bi-Polar):** A rapid manic-depressive cycle in which they move between the two extreme states of depression and overstimulation.

When any of these abnormal mood states are present, the physical, psychological, and social balance mechanisms either have broken down or were inherently inadequate to meet the stresses or challenges encountered.

So, how do you know if you're suffering from depression, mania, or manic-depression? Fortunately, it's fairly easy to determine by reviewing a list of symptoms and comparing those symptoms to what you're experiencing in your life. Let's take a moment to briefly review those symptom checklists.

2-9. Symptoms of Depression

The DSM-IV-TR, which is the standard diagnostic reference guide for psychiatrists, psychologists, and therapists, gives a compressive list of the symptoms of depression. I have modified this symptom list and added several questions that can help you identify if you should be concerned about suicidal ideation. The questionnaire is easy to use, ***but it is not a diagnostic instrument***. Your answers can help you determine if you may be suffering from depression, but you will need to see a psychiatrist or mental-health professional to confirm the diagnosis and develop a treatment plan that will work for you. Take a moment to complete the questionnaire.

Depression Symptom Checklist—DSM-IV-TR

Yes	No	1.	Do you feel sad or empty most of the day nearly every day? *(Major Depressive Episode—Criterion #1)*
Yes	No	2.	Would other people tend to say that you look sad, tearful, or lethargic most of the day nearly every day? *(Major Depressive Episode—Criterion #1)*
Yes	No	3.	Has the amount of interest or pleasure that you receive from doing all or most of your activities significantly decreased most of the day nearly every day? *(Major Depressive Episode—Criterion #2)*
Yes	No	4.	Would other people tend to say that you're not as interested in or don't enjoy what you're doing the way you used to? *(Major Depressive Episode— Criterion #2)*
Yes	No	5.	Have you lost your appetite or interest in eating? *(Major Depressive Episode—Criterion #3)*
Yes	No	6.	Have you recently lost a significant amount of weight (more than 5 percent of your total body weight) without dieting? *(Major Depressive Episode—Criterion #3)*
Yes	No	7.	Has your appetite significantly increased, causing you to overeat? *(Major Depressive Episode— Criterion #3—implied)*
Yes	No	8.	Have you recently gained a significant amount of weight (more than 5 percent of your total body weight) without wanting to? *(Major Depressive Episode—Criterion #3)*
Yes	No	9.	Do you have difficulty falling asleep, staying asleep throughout the night, or waking up early without feeling rested? This is called insomnia. *(Major Depressive Episode—Criterion #4)*
Yes	No	10.	Do you tend to sleep too much, sleep for extremely long periods of time, be unable to awaken and become active in the morning or when you have important activities to complete, and feel constantly tired and fatigued despite sleeping a lot? This is

			called hypersomnia. *(Major Depressive Episode—Criterion #4)*
Yes	No	11.	Do you tend to feel so restless or agitated that other people can tell how upset you are by observing you? *(Major Depressive Episode—Criterion #5)*
Yes	No	12.	Do you tend to feel so slowed down and lethargic that other people can tell how little energy you have by observing you? *(Major Depressive Episode—Criterion #5)*
Yes	No	13.	Do you feel tired, fatigued, and without energy most of the day nearly every day? *(Major Depressive Episode—Criterion #6)*
Yes	No	14.	Do you tend to feel worthless, useless, ashamed, and guilty much of the day nearly every day? *(Major Depressive Episode—Criterion #7)*
Yes	No	15.	Have you started to have problems thinking clearly, paying attention to things that used to interest you, or making decisions that used to come easily to you? *(Major Depressive Episode—Criterion #7)*
Yes	No	16.	Have other people noticed that you are having problems thinking clearly, paying attention to things that used to interest you, or making decisions that used to come easily to you? *(Major Depressive Episode—Criterion #7)*
Yes	No	17.	Have you started to feel that life is not worth living, have persistent thoughts about death and dying, feel that you would be better off dead, or wished you could die? *(These are recurrent thoughts about death—Major Depressive Episode—Criterion #9)*
Yes	No	18.	Have you thought about killing yourself, developed a specific plan to kill yourself, assembled the things needed to kill yourself, or attempted suicide? *(These are symptoms of suicidal ideation—Major Depressive Episode—Criterion #9)*

So, how do you make sense out of your answers? If you have experienced five or more of the above symptoms persistently for a two-week period, you may be suffering from a major depressive episode and should consider a professional evaluation. If you answered "yes" to question 17 or 18, you should call someone for help as soon as possible and put together a plan to protect you from the risk of suicide.

2-10. Symptoms of Mania

Because depression is often part of a disorder called manic-depressive illness, it is important to be able to make a distinction between the symptoms of depression and the symptoms of mania. The following symptoms of mania were listed by the National Institute of Mental Health (NIMH) in its publication titled *Depression*. (NIMH 2000, 2002) I've also converted this list into a simple questionnaire. Just place a check in front of the symptoms that apply to you.

		Mania Symptoms Checklist—Short Form
	1.	Do you frequently feel an excessive sense of elation?
	2.	Do you have regular episodes of strong or unusual irritability?
	3.	Do you go through periods of time when you have a decreased need for sleep?
	4.	Do you have grandiose thoughts?
	5.	Do you have periods of time when you talk excessively, ramble, or have a difficult time not talking?
	6.	Do you have periods of time where your mind starts racing and you can't turn off your thoughts?

	7.	Do you experience periods of time when you have an increased sexual desire or feel a compulsion to act out sexually in inappropriate ways?
	8.	Do you experience periods of time when you have a markedly increased sense of energy?
	9.	Do you experience periods of time when you have used poor judgment or do self-destructive things because of your excessive feelings or energy?
	10.	Do you experience periods of time when you have to do things around other people that you later feel were inappropriate or that later caused you to feel embarrassed or ashamed?

Part 3.
Biopsychosocial
Model of Depression

Depression, and its close cousins mania and manic depression, can be thought of as biopsychosocial disorders. In other words, each disorder consists of a complex set of biological, psychological, and social symptoms that interact together to create and maintain the depression, the mania, or the manic-depressive mood swings. In this book I'm going to focus primarily on depression, but much of the information and recovery techniques can be applied to recovery from mania and manic-depressive illness as well.

By viewing depression in a biopsychosocial frame of reference, all contributing factors can be considered and a comprehensive recovery plan can be developed that deals with all levels of symptoms. Let's examine the biological, psychological, and social symptoms of depression more closely.

3-1. Factors that Influence Depression

Although depression is one of the most common mental-health problems, the definitive cause of depressive illness is not fully known. A great deal of progress has been made in understanding the biopsychosocial factors that can cause depression, yet it is clear that different types of depression may have different causes. It is also clear that there are gender and age-related factors that can influence the development of depression. As a result, for the purpose of this book, I will talk about *factors that influence the development of depression* rather than factors that cause depression.

Family History: Some types of depression run in families, suggesting that a biological vulnerability can be genetically inherited. Genetic studies of people with bipolar disorder and their immediate family members found that the family members with bipolar disorder have a somewhat different genetic makeup than those who do not get ill. However, the reverse is not true: Not everybody with the genetic makeup that causes vulnerability to bipolar disorder will have the illness. Apparently additional factors, possibly stresses at home, work, or school, are involved in its onset.

In some families, major depression also seems to occur generation after generation. However, it can also occur in people who have no family history of depression.

Brain Chemistry Changes: Whether inherited or not, major depressive disorder is often associated with changes in brain structures or brain function.

Psychological Factors: People who have low self-esteem, who consistently view themselves and the world with pessimism or who are readily over-whelmed by stress, are prone to depression. Whether this represents a psychological predisposition or an early form of the illness is not clear.

Physical Illness: Serious physical illness can trigger a major depressive episode. This is because extreme physical changes in the body can be accompanied by brain-chemistry changes that affect mental and emotional functioning. Medical illnesses such as stroke, heart attack, cancer, Parkinson's disease, hormonal disorders, and pain disorders can cause depressive illness. The onset of depression can make a sick person apathetic. The depression takes away their motivation to participate in treatment, manage their illness, and take care of themselves physically, psychologically, socially, and spiritually. As a result, a person with severe depression may be unwilling to follow through with treatment for their health-care problem. This can prolong their recovery period, contribute to relapse, and lead to secondary health-care problems.

Stress, Grief, and Loss: Any stressful life change that causes high stress, grief, or loss can influence the development of depression. This includes such things as the death of a loved one, divorce, the loss of a job, relationship problems, and financial problems. Any stressful change in life patterns can trigger a depressive episode. This includes positive changes that increase stress. Many people develop depression after getting promoted to a better job, moving to a different part of the country where they have wanted to move for years, or getting married to someone they know and love.

Combined Factors: Most people suffering from serious depression have a variety of related factors that contribute to their depression. A combination of genetic, psychological, and environmental factors are involved in the onset of a depressive disorder. Most people experience a sequence of problems that increases stress and builds in a cumulative pattern. At some point their ability to physically and psychologically cope with the progressive problems breaks down. The result can be the onset of a major depressive illness.

3-2. Biological Factors in Depression

Biological depression results from an abnormal response of the brain and nervous system to internal and external events. This abnormal response can be called a *depressive brain response*. When people have a depressive brain response their nervous system doesn't respond normally to things that happen. The brain fails to produce a sufficient amount of a neurotransmitter called serotonin. The low levels of serotonin lead to an inhibited brain response that tends to create feelings of depression.

Some people may be genetically predisposed to experience depression. Other people may be born with normal brain-chemistry systems but experience high levels of debilitating stress, abuse, or trauma that interfere with or damage the normal brain-chemistry systems that regulate depression. These experiences can create physiological tendencies toward depression. Other people may use, abuse, or become addicted to alcohol or other drugs. Depression is a common symptom in the early stages of recovery from addiction. The depression can be caused, in large part, by the biological affects of alcohol and other drugs on the brain.

Antidepressant medications can be a helpful adjunct to treatment for people suffering from forms of depression that have a strong biological basis. There are a variety of different antidepressant medications that we'll discuss in detail later in the book.

Biological Factors in Depression

1. Genetic Predisposition
2. Stress-Impaired Brain Functioning
3. Effects of Alcohol or Other Drugs

At this point, there is one important thing to remember: antidepressant medication alone is only a part of treatment of depression. From a biopsychosocial perspective, it becomes clear that physiological interventions alone are not and cannot be the total answer for depression. As you will clearly see, the most effective way to recover from depression is to use medication along with psychological and social therapies.

3-3. Psychological Factors in Depression

Psychologically, depression seems to be associated with specific mental events. Four psychological systems interact with each other to influence depression. These are the *cognitive system*, which mediates thinking, the *affective system*, which mediates feelings and emotions, the *imagery system*, which links pre-verbal or nonverbal activity of the brain and nervous system to the thinking and emotional processes, and the *behavioral system*, which mediates urges and actions. Let's look at each of these in more detail.

Psychological Systems that Influence Depression

1. **Cognitive System**—Mediates thinking
2. **Affective System**—Mediates feelings and emotions
3. **Imagery System**—Links nonverbal brain activity to thinking and emotional processes
4. **Behavioral System**—Mediates urges and actions

Depressive Thinking

People who get depressed tend to think in ways that make them feel depressed. They have a negative view of themselves and tend to interpret things in negative, pessimistic, demoralizing, or catastrophic ways.

Core Depressive Thoughts

1. I am a defective human being!
2. My life is terrible and awful!
3. I am helpless!
4. I am hopeless!
5. Nothing can ever change!

Depressive thinking happens quietly in our mind. We say things to ourselves and actually carry on inner conversations with ourselves. Depressive thinking begins when we start believing that we are defective human beings and that our lives are terrible and awful. Then our depressive thinking can kick into full gear as we start telling ourselves that we are helpless, hopeless, and unable to change. As a result, we can get creative and build a lot of variety into the ways of thinking that cause our depression and make it feel like we're trapped with no way out.

There were two men living in a rural village during medieval times. Modrid tended to use depressive thinking and as a result tended to get easily depressed. Wil, on the other hand, was resilient and was rarely depressed. Wil owned a single horse, which he kept in his corral. One day his horse broke out of the corral and ran away.

"That's terrible," said Modrid, who got very upset.

"Maybe yes and maybe no," said Wil. "Time will tell." He then calmly started to repair the corral fence.

The next day Wil's horse returned leading three wild horses back into the corral. Because the fence was now fixed, Wil closed the gate and had four horses instead of one.

"That's great," said Modrid, who became extremely excited and cheerful as a result of Wil's luck. "This will make everything better."

"Maybe yes and maybe no," said Wil. "Time will tell." Then he started to think about how he was going to feed and train the new horses.

The next day Wil's son was thrown from one of the wild horses he was trying to break and broke his leg when he hit the fence.

"That awful," said Modrid, as he started feeling depressed because of the bad luck of his friend's son.

"Maybe yes and maybe no," said Wil. "Time will tell." He then went about tending to his son by putting a cast on his broken leg.

The next day the local general in charge of the king's army came into town and drafted all of the young men into the army to go off and fight a war. Wil's son was left behind because he had a broken leg and couldn't travel or fight.

"That's great," said Modrid, as he once again became elated.

"Maybe yes and maybe no," said Wil as he planned to get up early to do the chores his son used to do.

Here are some forms that depressive thinking can take:

1. **Negative View of Self:** When we're using depressive thinking we tend to say negative and insulting things to ourselves about ourselves. Here are some of the depressive thoughts that can become automatic and habitual:

    a. I am defective, inadequate, diseased, or deprived.

    b. I have unpleasant experiences because I am defective as a human being.

    c. Because I am defective as a human being I am worthless and undesirable to others.

    d. I do not have what it takes to be happy or content in life.

    e. The only way to survive is to discount my abilities and constantly criticize myself.

2. **Negative Interpretation of Experience:** As people move through their lives they experience many different things. They develop a set of decision rules for assigning meaning and value to the things that they experience. These rules for interpreting the events in our lives have a significant affect on our emotional well-being. When we're using depressive thinking we have a tendency to interpret our experiences in negative ways. Resilient people who are resistant to depression tend to think about things that happen to them in a more positive and optimistic way. Depressed people tend to use the following decision rules in assigning meaning to day-to-day experiences:

70

a. This proves that the world isn't fair.
b. This proves that the world is placing exorbitant demands on me.
c. This proves that the world is putting unfair obstacles in my path.
d. This proves that I have been defeated and that I can never win.
e. This proves that I am deprived and that I can never have what I need in order to have meaning, purpose, and happiness in my life.

3. **Negative View of the Future:** People who are suffering from depression tend to have the following negative views of the future:

a. My current problems will never be solved and will go on forever.
b. I will always feel the pain that I am feeling now.
c. Things will never get better.
d. Life will always be too hard for me to handle.
e. I will always be deprived of what I need to be happy.
f. I will always feel deeply frustrated.
g. I will always be alone and cut off from other people.
h. No one will ever understand me or be there for me.
i. No matter how hard I try, I will always fail.

Core Depressive Beliefs

There are a number of core depressive beliefs that influence the overall worldview of people suffering from depression. I've picked the nine most common to review. As you read the list, notice how just thinking these thoughts can start bringing you down. The more strongly you believe each of these thoughts is true, the more depressed you will probably become.

1. **Self:** I am defective. I don't have what it takes to be happy or content in life.

> How convinced are you that the above statement is true?
> Very Convinced   Convinced   Not Very Convinced   Not At All Convinced

2. **I am trapped and helpless.** My current problems are overwhelming me and there is no way out. There is nothing that I can do to feel better or to make things better.

> How convinced are you that the above statement is true?
> Very Convinced   Convinced   Not Very Convinced   Not At All Convinced

3. **I am hopeless.** My problems will never be solved. Things will never change. I will always be the way I am. There is no hope of improvement.

> How convinced are you that the above statement is true?
> Very Convinced   Convinced   Not Very Convinced   Not At All Convinced

4. **Self:** I am defective and don't have what it takes to handle my problems and to be happy in life.

> How convinced are you that the above statement is true?
> Very Convinced   Convinced   Not Very Convinced   Not At All Convinced

5. **Others:** Other people either don't care or they are incapable of doing anything that can help me.

> How convinced are you that the above statement is true?
> Very Convinced   Convinced   Not Very Convinced   Not At All Convinced

6. **The World:** The world doesn't treat me fairly.

> How convinced are you that the above statement is true?
> Very Convinced   Convinced   Not Very Convinced   Not At All Convinced

7. **The Past:** Nothing has ever gone right for me.

> How convinced are you that the above statement is true?
> Very Convinced   Convinced   Not Very Convinced   Not At All Convinced

8. **The Present:** There is nothing in my current life that is going right.

> How convinced are you that the above statement is true?
> Very Convinced   Convinced   Not Very Convinced   Not At All Convinced

9. **The Future:** Nothing will ever go right for me in the future.

> How convinced are you that the above statement is true?
> Very Convinced   Convinced   Not Very Convinced   Not At All Convinced

3-4. Social Factors in Depression

When we get depressed we tend to lose interest in other people. We become self-absorbed and tend to shrink our world to the size of a mud puddle. Even depressed people are capable of managing a mud puddle. When you're depressed, everything just seems like it's too much trouble.

People who make demands on you are viewed as too much trouble so you have a tendency to avoid them or push them away. You tend to attract and feel attracted to people who will buy into your depression, leave you alone, take care of things, and stop putting demands on you to function normally. When we're depressed it's as if we start walking around with a sign hanging from our neck that says, "Leave me alone! Expect nothing from me! I'm worthless and useless. You're too much trouble."

When other people read this message they have three basic choices: (1) They can leave us alone. If this happens we become isolated. (2) They can tell us we're wrong, ignore our depression, and expect us to just go back to the way things were. If this happens we get into conflicts, lose, and tend to get beaten into the ground. This makes our depression worse. (3) They can enable our depression by doing everything for us and expecting nothing in return. This allows everyone involved to pretend the depression doesn't exist while centering all aspects of life around our depression.

In healthy relationships, all people recognize when depression becomes a problem. They talk about what is happening and they work together to seek help.

Part 4: Cycle of Depression

Cognitive therapy has demonstrated that there is a link between what we think and how we feel. There is also a link between what we do and how we feel. This leads us to an important point: *If we start feeling depressed, then we must be thinking some depressive thoughts.*

As we discussed earlier, this process is called *depressive thinking* and is generally based on *depressive-thinking errors* that lead a person to believe that they are powerless, helpless, and have little ability to impact or change themselves or their lives.

If we start feeling depressed, then we must be thinking some depressive thoughts that lead us to believe that we are powerless, helpless, and have little ability to impact or change ourselves or our lives.

These depressive thoughts do not occur in isolation. They are linked with *depressive images* of past events or *depressive fantasies* of future outcomes that reinforce the thinking errors. The process goes like this:

Something happens that activates a depressive-thinking error. Our imagery system responds to this error in thinking by providing vivid sensory images of past experiences and projected future occurrences that support the thinking error. Our feeling system responds to the imagery by creating brain-chemistry changes (such as lower serotonin levels) that depress our mood. As we start feeling depressed we use this feeling as evidence that our depressive-thinking errors are, in fact, correct. This process is called *emotional reasoning* and is based on the mistaken belief, *"If I feel this way, it must be true."*

In this way, the depression creates an urge to stop trying and a desire to withdraw from the situations or relationships that are the focus of the depressive thinking. If we act on these urges, we reduce the stimulation through social withdrawal that reinforces the brain chemistry state associated with depression. We start feeling bored and lonely because there's nothing to do and no one to talk to. As we get more isolated, there are few opportunities to talk about what is happening and test our personal reality against someone else's point of view. This lack of reality testing further reinforces the depressive physiology, and the depression continues to intensify as a result of the progressive cycle.

In some cases, the depression begins with physiological factors that depress the nervous system and result in a diminished ability to respond. In other cases, the depression results from the habitual use of ways of thinking and behaving that are based on a fundamental assumption of helplessness, frustration, and powerlessness to make a change or to impact life or the world. In still other cases, people are caught up in legitimately stressful and often catastrophic events that lead to stress degeneration and then to depression. Most of us have two or more of these causative factors which are linked together to create the depression.

Here's another point to remember: Once you're suffering from a serious depression, it's time to declare an emergency and get help. It's a waste of time to squander your limited energy trying to figure out what caused your depression and who is to blame. If you don't take action, your depression will probably keep getting worse. Why? It's because of the self-reinforcing cycle of depression.

4-1. Self-Reinforcing Cycle of Depression

The biological and psychological symptoms of depression work together to create a self-reinforcing cycle that makes the depression more severe. These symptoms cause changes in what we think, feel, and do that tends to support and exaggerate the biological changes in the brain. In other words, the biological changes in brain chemistry caused by depression support self-defeating ways of thinking, managing feelings and emotions, and behaving that tend to make the depression get worse. As a result, a self-reinforcing cycle is created. As the biochemistry of depression gets worse, the tendency to think depressive thoughts, manage feelings and emotions in ways that increase depression, and behave in ways that create progressive and potentially depressing life problems increases.

As the behavioral changes associated with depression become more severe, the symptoms of depression begin to interfere with individual and family functioning. The person with a depressive disorder is often unable to fulfill their responsibilities as spouse or parent and may be unable to carry out their usual job responsibilities. This creates social problems that are processed through the depressive ways of thinking, managing feelings, and behaving, which in turn tends to aggravate the underlying depressive biochemistry. As a result, an out-of-control cycle that links biological, psychological, and social factors to the escalating symptoms of depression tends to develop. The end result can be a feeling of hopelessness.

4-2: The Core Hopelessness Syndrome

A key factor that distinguishes a normal period of sadness from a depressive episode is the presence of a core hopelessness syndrome. To understand the concept of a core hopelessness syndrome, we must first examine the concept of *hope* and *hopelessness* and then look at the definition of a *syndrome*.

The Concept of Hope: Hope is the belief that things will turn out for the best. It is the felt-sense experience or emotion that accompanies the belief that everything will somehow be OK. Hope is built on a foundation of psychological processes such as faith, rational thinking, problem solving, detachment, and acceptance. Hope can be defined in different ways. I'd like to provide a variety of definitions of hope. Read the following list and see which definition most strongly resonates with you:

1. Hope is the belief or conviction that something good is possible and will probably occur.
2. Hope is the emotional reaction that occurs in response to the belief that something good is possible and will occur.
3. Hope is the psychological process of both desiring and anticipating an outcome with the strong expectation or belief that it is possible to obtain it. To desire something means to want it. To anticipate something means to expect that it will happen.
4. Hope is an inner process that causes us to want something good, to believe that it is possible to get it, and to expect with some degree of certainty that we will get it.
5. Hope is the process of developing a sense of knowing within one's own mind that a desired outcome will, in fact, occur at some time in the future.

Psychological Processes Associated with Hope: These definitions suggest that *hope as a psychological process* is intimately connected with the processes of purpose, desire, self-motivation, goal setting, action planning, and determination.

1. *Purpose* is the process of knowing that there is something important for you to do, have, or be.
2. *Desire* is emotion that creates a focused energy for accomplishing your purpose.
3. *Self-motivation* is the ability to generate the inner energy and commitment necessary to take action to get what is desired.
4. *Goal Setting* is the process of setting a goal and establishing a firm commitment to achieve it.

5. *Action Planning* is the process of developing the steps that can be taken to produce the desired outcome.
6. *Determination* is the process of developing or sustaining a commitment to produce the desired outcome despite problems, obstacles, and setbacks.

Notice that these processes are linked together in a continuum. First, I must have a purpose or something important that I take responsibility for doing or being. Second, I must have a desire that is strong enough to create the motivation and energy needed to accomplish my purpose. Third, I must set a goal. I must figure out a concrete way in which I can act on my purpose. Fourth, I must motivate myself to take action. Nothing can be accomplished except through mental effort and physical action. Fifth, I must develop a plan that will move me to the accomplishment of my goal. Sixth, I must have the determination to keep myself going despite obstacles and setbacks.

It has been my experience that most people who are depressed have become disconnected from their personal sense of meaning and purpose. Nothing seems worth doing. There is nothing worth the investment of time and energy. In other words, most depressed people have lost hope—they have come to believe that they and their circumstances are hopeless.

The Concept of Hopelessness: Hopelessness is the belief that there is no way out. It is the belief that no matter what I do, it won't be enough to achieve my goals. In its worst manifestation, hopelessness is the belief that there is no goal that is worth striving for.

Hopelessness is the opposite of hope or hopefulness. As a result, it can be defined as follows:

- Hopelessness is the belief that things will *not* turn out for the best and will, in fact, turn out for the worst.

- Hopelessness is the felt-sense experience or emotion that accompanies this negative belief.

- Hopelessness is the absence of the psychological processes that create and sustain hope (namely purpose, desire, self-motivation, goal setting, action planning, and determination).

- Hopelessness is the presence of the psychological processes that destroy hope (namely purposeless, apathy or the lack of desire, complacency or the lack of motivation, aimlessness or the lack of goal setting, passivity or the lack of action planning, and immobilization or the lack of determination).

Psychological Processes Associated with Hopelessness

These definitions suggest that hopelessness, like hope, is a psychological process that is intimately connected with the processes of purposelessness, apathy (lack of desire), loss of motivation, loss of meaningful goals, absence of a plan, and a lack of energy or determination to try to find a solution (lethargy).

- *Purposelessness* is the process of convincing ourselves that there is nothing important for us to do, have, or be.

- *Apathy (Lack of Desire)* is the emotion that drains us of energy and keeps us from identifying or trying to accomplish our primary purpose.

81

- **Loss of Motivation** is the inability to generate the inner energy and commitment needed to take action to get what is desired. In extreme forms, it is the inability to feel a desire to accomplish anything.

- **Loss of Meaningful Goals** is the inability to identify goals that seem important and the unwillingness to make a firm commitment to achieve a goal once it is identified. For a goal to be meaningful, we must make a decision to empower the goal with a sense of personal importance. It is the decision that this thing is important—it needs to be done and I am the only one or the best one to do it.

- **Absence of a Plan** occurs when people refuse to invest time and energy in seeking alternative solutions to known problems or in seeking out some meaningful goal to achieve or problem to solve.

- **Lethargy** is a lack of energy or determination. It is the inability to find the energy to invest in resolving a problem, achieving a goal, or seeking out something of meaning that can give purpose to life.

And so hopelessness, like hope, is a belief or conviction. It is also an inner process that creates a felt-sense experience or emotion. We can also define hopelessness on five different levels:

1. Hopelessness is the *belief that there is either no desirable outcome or that a desired outcome is not obtainable* and, in fact, will not occur.

2. Hopelessness is the *belief or strong conviction that a desired outcome is impossible or unobtainable* no matter what is done.

3. Hopelessness is the *emotional reaction that occurs in response to the belief* that there is either no desirable outcome or that a desired outcome is not obtainable and, in fact, will not occur.
4. Hopelessness is the *psychological process of both wanting or needing an outcome to occur along with the belief that it will never occur.*
5. Hopelessness is the *process of coming to believe that a desired outcome will never occur and that there is nothing one can do to make it occur.*

Hopelessness is an inner process that causes us to stop doing five things. Hopelessness stops us from:
1. believing that we deserve to have things of value in our lives;
2. wanting to have things of value in our lives;
3. believing that it is impossible to get things of value even if we were to want them;
4. believing that it is possible to enjoy things of value even if we were able to have them; and
5. expecting to have things of value in our lives.

Research indicates that in all depressed and suicidal patients there is a central core of psychological beliefs that contributes to the depression and supports the irrational belief that there is no way out or that suicide is the only way to manage their problems. The psychological core of depression and suicide is *hopelessness.*

4-3. Recovery Is Possible

There is good news. There are effective treatments for depression that combine antidepressant medications with other biopsychosocial treatments that can help 80 percent of those who are suffering from depression. With adequate ongoing biopsycho-social treatment, future depression episodes may be prevented or reduced in duration and severity.

Unfortunately, current evidence indicates that nearly two out of three depressed people do not seek treatment and suffer needlessly. Many people seeking help for depression receive only partial treatment in the form of antidepressant medication. They rarely have access to the proven psychosocial treatments that alone or in combination with antidepressant medications can drastically increase recovery from depression and reduce relapse rates.

Many people in recovery from addiction get the misinformation that antidepressant medications are addictive and should be avoided at all costs. In my experience, this can be a dangerous belief.

Antidepressants are powerful medications and can be harmful if not properly managed. This is true for most medications, including insulin. Give insulin to a diabetic who needs it and it works wonders. Give the same dose to nondiabetics and it can make them sick or kill them. The same is true for antidepressants.

If antidepressants are properly prescribed and monitored by a doctor who understands both addiction and depression, they can be safely used. It's always best to make the use of antidepressant medication part of a total recovery program that includes addiction counseling, cognitive therapy for depression, and involvement in recovery support groups. Later in this book we'll spend an entire section talking about antidepressant medication so that you can make an informed choice.

Part 5: Depression and Other Disorders

Research has shown that depression often co-oc-curs with other medical, psychiatric, and addictive disorders. Unfortunately, many medical and psychiatric professionals don't screen their patients for depression. As a result, the depression can be unrecognized with no treatment being recommended. This can lead to the continuation of severe symptoms of depression that can lead to relapse, to addiction, psychiatric problems, and medical disorders.

5-1. Medical Conditions and Depression

The medical conditions that are frequently associated with depression include stroke, heart disease, cancer, diabetes, and a variety of other lifestyle-related health problems, especially those resulting in chronic pain. The rate of major depression among those with medical illnesses is significant, ranging from 5 to 10 percent among outpatients receiving medical treatment and 10 to 14 percent among medical inpatients receiving inpatient care.

Research has shown that major depression occurs in between 40 and 65 percent of patients who have had a myocardial infarction (MI). They may also have a shorter life expectancy than nondepressed MI patients. Depression also occurs in approximately 25 percent of cancer patients and between 10 and 27 percent of post-stroke patients.

Depressed feelings can be a common reaction to many medical illnesses. In most cases, the depression is mild to moderate and lasts only a short time. As a result, the reports of depression in medical patients may be minimized and not get the serious attention they deserve.

Failure to recognize and treat depression that is co-occurring with medical disorders may result in increased impairment and diminished improvement in physical recovery. In serious life-threatening illnesses, depression can lower resiliency in the face of treatment setbacks, diminish the will to live, and contribute to higher rates of death than would normally be expected.

Proper diagnosis and treatment of co-occurring depression may bring benefits to the patient through improved medical status, enhanced quality of life, a reduction in the degree of pain and disability, and improved treatment compliance and cooperation.

5-2. Mental Health Problems and Depression

The mental health problems and psychiatric disorders that are frequently associated with depression include anxiety disorders, panic disorders, eating disorders, post-traumatic stress disorders (PTSD), and sexual disorders.

There is a higher than average co-occurrence of depression with other psychiatric disorders, such as anxiety and eating disorders. Concurrent depression is present in 13 percent of patients with panic disorder. In about 25 percent of these patients, the panic disorder preceded the depressive disorder. Between 50 and 75 percent of eating-disorder patients (anorexia nervosa and bulimia) have a lifetime history of major depressive disorder. In such cases, detection of depression can help clarify the initial diagnosis and may result in more effective treatment and a better outcome for the patient.

5-3. Addiction and Depression

As we mentioned in the first part of the book on addiction, depression often co-occurs with the use, abuse, and addiction to alcohol and other mood-altering drugs. Depression can contribute to the start of an addiction, prevent people from getting early treatment for addiction, increase the risk of suicide, and contribute to high rates of relapse.

Substance-use disorders (both alcohol and other substances) frequently co-occur with depression. Substance-use disorders are present in 32 percent of individuals with depressive disorders. They co-occur in 27 percent of those with major depression and 56 percent of those with bipolar disorder.

Depression can contribute to the start of an addiction when depressed people begin using alcohol or other drugs in an attempt to self-medicate the symptoms of depression.

Depression can also prevent people from getting early treatment for addiction. An addicted person with severe depression can become lethargic and lose a sense of optimism and hope. As a result, their motivation to get help of any kind tends to decrease. When addicts with serious depression enter treatment, they often drop out before completing it because the symptoms of depression are not recognized or treated in many addiction programs.

The high rate of suicide that occurs among people with addictive disorders could well be a by-product of the high rate of undetected depression among addicted people.

Depression, if not identified and properly treated during the recovery process from addiction, can contribute to high rates of relapse. The depressed person in recovery is clean and sober and is doing everything recommended to achieve recovery. Their depression, however, continues to get worse and they don't understand why. Unless the depression is identified and treated, its symptoms can trigger addictive thinking and eventual relapse. The renewed use of alcohol or other drugs is often an attempt to self-medicate the depressive symptoms.

Substance use must be discontinued in order to clarify the diagnoses and maximize the effectiveness of psychiatric interventions. Treatment for depression as a separate condition is necessary if the depression remains after the substance-use problem has ended.

Part 6: Recovery from Depression— A Brief Guide

In the last half of this book we're going to cover a lot of information about what you can do to identify and successfully manage your symptoms. There are many things you can try. Some of the things will work, some won't, and the whole process will take time. Those who drop out in the middle of the process often relapse and have to start all over again.

In this section of the book I want to explain three things:

1. The stages of recovery from depression so you understand the long term process it takes to recover;
2. ten simple, but not easy, things you can do to start feeling better right now; and
3. how to involve your family and friends in a way that will help your recovery while repairing the important relationships that make life worth living.

6-1. Stages of Recovery from Depression

According to the American Psychiatric Association (APA) the treatment of depression consists of three phases. I've adapted the language of these phases to make them a little easier to understand, but the APA has mapped out the progressive process of recovery.

Phase 0: Active Depression: This phase actually occurs before recovery begins. During this stage, we develop serious symptoms of depression that begin to interfere with our lives. Unfortunately, most of us don't understand what depression is and how it works. Many of us are working an addiction recovery program and believe that should fix everything. And so as our depression gets worse we just work our program harder. Then we start getting discouraged when it doesn't work. We know something is wrong but we blame it all on our addiction and develop a strong denial that anything else may be going on. Eventually we start to get desperate because no matter what we do things keep getting worse instead of better.

Phase 1: Stabilization: During this phase, we enter treatment, complete an evaluation, and start working to stabilize our most severe symptoms of depression. The major weapons in this battle are: (1) a recommitment to our addiction recovery program; (2) cognitive therapy for depression; and (3) a daily structure of supportive activities and, if necessary, the use of antidepressant medication. The primary focus is to learn how to identify the immediate biological, psychological, and social symptoms that are most disruptive, develop plans for managing those symptoms, and then adjusting those plans until they start to work for us. Depression is a disease.

The treatment of depression is both a science and an art. The science of depression treatment tells us the general things that can be helpful in managing, reducing, and eventually eliminating our symptoms. The art of depression treatment comes from applying the science-based principles to real, living, breathing human beings who want a life, not just a 24/7 recovery plan.

The stabilization can take anywhere from two to six months depending on whether medication is prescribed, how people react to the medication, whether or not they are participating in a cognitive therapy program for depression, and how well they learn to integrate their recovery programs for addiction and depression.

Phase 2: Lifestyle and Personality Change: During this phase, activities are prescribed that reinforce and enhance the initial progress. This usually involves a number of things: practicing techniques for managing depressive thoughts, feelings, and actions until they become an automatic habit; straightening out our relationships that have been damaged by the depression. This can involve meeting with a counselor to redefine the basic dynamics of the relationships. It's important that everyone knows where they stand and what they have the right to expect of the person with depression and what areas of special support are appropriate and necessary.

Phase 3: Maintenance Phase: During this phase, a relapse prevention plan is established to allow the person to recognize the early warning signs that depression may be returning. This usually involves an ongoing program of recovery activities and a list of relapse warning signs that tend to precede a relapse into serious depression. It is interesting to note that the American Psychiatric Association recommends both psychotherapy and medication management. The specific form of psychotherapy most frequently used is **Cognitive Therapy for Depression**, which focuses on identifying and changing the major addictive thoughts, feelings, and behaviors that tend to create and maintain symptoms.

6-2. Ten Guidelines for Starting Depression Recovery

I want to start out by providing some general guidelines about what you can do to begin managing your depression more successfully. The place to begin is by looking directly at your beliefs about being hopeful or hopeless.

Depressive disorders make one feel exhausted, worthless, helpless, and hopeless. Negative thoughts and feelings make some people feel like giving up. It is important to realize that these negative views are part of the depression and typically do not accurately reflect the actual circumstances. Negative thinking will begin to fade as you begin to make small decisions and take small steps each day to recover from depression and protect your sobriety. Here is a list of ten things you can start to do right now to feel a little better. Remember, recovery from depression is like walking up a down escalator. There is no such thing as standing still. You will either force yourself to do a number of small things each day to feel a little bit better or your disease of depression, complicated by your old addictive thinking, will make you feel worse.

It's important to be aware that you probably will not feel like doing any of the ten suggestions that follow. When you're suffering from depression, the depression has hijacked your brain and taken control of your motivational process. Your brain is sending false signals that tell you it's good to do things that make the depression worse. Your depression motivates you to do things like staying in bed, isolating yourself, being alone and inactive, and feeling sorry for yourself. These things are guaranteed to make your depression worse. Your depression will rebel against the idea of doing anything that could make you feel better. You won't want to do healthy things like get up at a set time each morning, follow a morning ritual to get yourself going and ready to face the world, spend time with other people, and schedule time to do small things that you enjoy doing. Your depression will tell you that these things are dumb or stupid. Your depression will tell you that you're too depressed to do any of these things.

Here's a little bit of good news: ***You are not your depression.*** You are the person who is depressed. Because you're not your depression you have a choice. You can choose to give in to the feelings of depression and shrink your life to a smelly little mud puddle. Or you can choose to fight back and do some simple little things each day that can make you feel just a little bit better. I can almost guarantee that you won't feel like doing these things. When depression hijacks the brain, little things become difficult to do. But remember, you have a choice—minute-to-minute choices that you are constantly making. That choice is either to give in to the feelings of depression, go with the flow, and do things that will make you feel a little bit worse or to break out of the pattern and force yourself to do little things that can make you feel a little bit better.

Here's a list of ten simple things you can do today to feel a little bit better.

1. **Start acting better even if you don't feel like it:** It's important to realize that you can't wait until your depression is gone to start doing something to recover. You need to start doing things to recover despite your depression. You won't start feeling better until you start thinking better and acting better. Your depression will decrease as a result of doing things to manage it more effectively. If you do nothing, your depression will probably keep getting worse.

In the Twelve-Step program, it is suggested that if we don't feel like doing something, we should "act as if" we feel like it and do it anyway. One thing is certain if you are depressed—you won't feel like doing the things you need to do to recover from your depression. Your depression has hijacked your brain and your brain is misfiring in ways that make you want to do things that will make you feel more depressed. These malfunctioning brain circuits also make you resist doing things that will help you manage your depression.

You will notice at AA meetings there is often a sign in the meeting rooms that says: *Think! Think! Think!* There is no sign that says *Feel! Feel! Feel!* This is because addiction causes your motivational system to malfunction. You need to force yourself to do things you don't want to do that are good for you. You also need to resist the urge to do things that are not good for you that you want to do. To do this you have to put Intellect (I) over Emotion (E). We learn what we need to do in recovery and force ourselves to do it whether we feel like it or not. This is called *putting I over E—putting intellect over emotion.*

> **You won't start feeling better until you start thinking better and acting better.**

2. **Set realistic goals that you are willing to accomplish despite your depression.** Managing your depression is your responsibility. The bad news is this: *Nobody is coming to save you.* The good news is: *You can choose to do things each day that can make you feel a little bit better.* The responsibility is yours. You have a choice. You can continue as you are and allow the slow downward spiral of your depression to continue, which will cause the depression to get worse and may lead to a relapse back into addiction. Or, you can choose to assert energy and mobilize social support to help you do things that will make you feel a little bit better. You can, for example, get up and go to Twelve-Step meetings. At the meetings, you can talk about the battle you're having with your depression. You can listen to others and try to hear things they did to help them deal with their depression. You can get up and go for short walks. You can call a friend. You can schedule activities to get you out of the house. You can tell your friends and family about your depression and your efforts to recover. You can ask them to help and assume a reasonable amount of responsibility.

Easy does it, but do it. Don't push yourself too hard or expect unrealistic results. On the other hand, don't just give in and do nothing but become an isolated couch potato who refuses to do anything all day long.

3. **Create a schedule of recovery activities and write it down.** Give yourself a definite time to get up in the morning and set an alarm clock. Sched-

95

ule a morning ritual that gets you up, showered, and dressed to face the day. Have something to do each morning, afternoon, and evening. Eat three healthy meals each day and take some extra vitamins and amino acid supplements.

4. **Break large tasks into small ones, set priorities, and do what you are able to do.** Recovery from depression is a lot like starting a weight training program. You start with light weights and work your way up to heavier weights. If you try to lift weights that are too heavy, you'll fail, become discouraged, and quit. Recovery from depression is similar in that you build strength slowly. Start by putting small, simple things that can make you feel better on your schedule every day. Then make a commitment to do them no matter how depressed you feel. Here's an example:

If you have trouble getting out of bed in the morning, set several alarm clocks and place them across the room. If you live with friends or family ask them to check on you to make sure you get up at the scheduled time.

You can break a big task into smaller tasks and activities. You can, for example, write out each activity of your morning ritual for getting up and ready for the day. Then you can check off each activity as you do it. Here is a sample list.

Morning Ritual to Get Up and Get Out of the House

1. Wake up and turn off the alarm clock
2. Get up whether I feel like it or not
3. Go to the bathroom and take a shower
4. Get dressed for the day
5. Read my daily meditation book
6. Write out my to do list and schedule or appointments for the day
7. Eat breakfast
8. Force myself to leave for my first activity or appointment whether I like it or not

5. **Don't isolate yourself—schedule time each day to be with other people.** This social time does not need to be complicated. Eat meals with the family whether you feel like it or not. Sit with others who are watching TV. Get to your Twelve-Step meetings a few minutes early and sit with some other people. Introduce yourself to people you don't know at meetings. Ask others to have coffee after a meeting. Watch or read the news every day so you have some current information for simple conversations

6. **Find someone you can talk to and confide in.** It's important to have someone you can talk to about how you feel. The great thing about the Twelve-Step program is that meetings give you a perfect opportunity to evaluate people by listening to their comments. The general culture supports openness and honesty. The principles of sponsorship give you a perfect chance to invite someone into a close relationship to help you apply the Steps to managing

both your addiction recovery and your depression. Don't wait until you feel like being with other people. Most depressed people prefer being alone and never feel like being with others. If you isolate and stay alone you'll end up getting more depressed and feeling worse. You have to be willing to act despite your depression. Force yourself to get up and be around people whether you want to or not.

7. **Participate in small activities each day that can make you feel better.** Make a list of the things you used to enjoy doing. Then put at least one of those activities on your daily schedule each day. These fun activities don't have to be complicated. Watch the sun go down. Go to a movie, or a ballgame, or participate in religious, social, or other activities that you used to enjoy. Buy a novel that you may find interesting and read it. Rent a video and watch it with the kids. The idea is to force yourself to do things that might distract you from your depression and give you a few minutes of enjoyment. Once again, don't wait until you want to do it. Your depression will make you want to shrink your life to a mud puddle and never do anything that is enjoyable. Force yourself to schedule these activities despite your depression.

8. **Do a little bit of mild exercise each day.** You don't have to train for the Olympics or a marathon. Just get yourself up and take a walk. Join the YMCA or a health club and go swimming two or three times a week. Even if you don't want to exercise, get a sweat suit and hang out at the gym or health club. Do a set or two on one of the machines or try the treadmill. You can participate in one of the gym's organized activities, like softball or aerobics. Any of these activities may help. Moderate exercise three

times a week for twenty to thirty minutes has been proven to significantly reduce depression.

9. **Expect your mood to improve gradually, not immediately.** In the Twelve-Step program, they say we seek "progress, not perfection." Feeling better takes time. Feeling better results from the long-term consequence of making small decisions each day to start thinking better and acting better despite feeling depressed. Remember that as an addicted person you'll tend to expect instant gratification. You will probably want to do one heroic effort at recovery from depression and then magically feel better. Your addictive thinking will tell you that if you can't get well quickly and with little effort, it's not worth doing anything. Challenge this thinking and prepare for small steps, expect slow and gradual progress, including periods of ups and downs in terms of the severity of depression. Don't get yourself unnecessarily upset about it. Try to detach and be philosophical about it. Yes, you're depressed and feel down, but it's not the end of the world. You can do little things each day that will either make you feel a little bit better or a little worse. The choice is yours. What happens in the long run will depend on the sum total of the small choices you make each and every day. It's not hopeless unless you decide it is.

10. **Postpone important decisions until your depression has lifted:** If possible, put off making important decisions until the depression has lifted. When you are depressed, your judgment is impaired. You will tend to be pessimistic and have a negative view of the future. It's important to find at least one or two trusted advisors with whom you can discuss important decisions. Try not to put yourself in the

position where you need to make decisions about significant life changes such as changing jobs, getting married or divorced, buying or selling houses, or making geographical moves to other parts of the country. If you absolutely need to make such decisions, discuss it with other people who know you well and have a more objective view of your situation. Remember, your depression will create feelings that will motivate you to make bad decisions. Depression is a parasitic illness that will do anything necessary to get you to make decisions that will allow it to grow. As a result, you probably won't feel like making the right decision. Your depression will motivate you to take the easy way out and make dumb decisions. Then when the decision blows up in your face it will be a cause for you to get more depressed and to further beat yourself up for doing such a dumb thing.

People rarely "snap out of" a depression. But they can feel a little better day by day. *Remember*, positive thinking will replace the negative thinking that is part of the depression and will disappear as your depression responds to treatment. You can start doing little things each day that will help you to feel a little better.

Here's a checklist of the ten things we just discussed. It may not be a bad idea to make a copy of it and put it somewhere so you will see it during the day. Remember, right now your depression is running your life. You have to start doing things to put the sober and responsible *you* back in charge. This means starting to do things every day even if you don't feel like it.

Ten Things You Can Do to Feel a Little Bit Better Today

1. Start acting better even if you don't feel like it—*act as if.*

2. Set realistic goals that you are willing to accomplish despite your depression.

3. Create a schedule of recovery activities and write it down.

4. Break large tasks into small ones, set priorities, and do what you are able to do.

5. Don't isolate yourself—schedule time each day to be with other people.

6. Find someone you can talk to and confide in.

7. Participate in small activities each day that can make you feel better.

8. Do a little bit of mild exercise each day.

9. Expect your mood to improve gradually, not immediately.

10. Postpone important decisions until your depression has lifted.

6-3. Let Your Family and Friends Help You

In all the research I've reviewed about depression, recovery, and relapse, one thing stands out to me. Your chances of successful recovery go up as you are willing and able to let other people get involved in your recovery. Both addiction and depression are illnesses that surround themselves by walls of shame, guilt, and isolation. *Shame* results from the mistaken belief that we are addicted and depressed because we are somehow defective as people. *Guilt* results from the mistaken belief that we became addicted and are currently depressed because we have done something wrong. *Isolation* results from the belief that we must hide our shame and guilt from others. If we buy into these mistaken beliefs and allow ourselves to wallow in shame and guilt, our depression will get worse and we'll isolate ourselves from others. We'll accept the mistaken belief that we are defective and unacceptable to others and use that belief as an excuse to push other people out of our lives.

It's important to fight back against this tendency by inviting other people in. To do this you need to know how to teach other people what is helpful and what's not. That's why I've prepared a list of guidelines for how you can invite family members and friends to become part of your recovery. If you follow these guidelines, you will probably find yourself renegotiating your relationships in a healthier and more honest way. This will help relieve a lot of stress and pressure that may be contributing to your depression and toward addiction relapse. Here are those guidelines:

1. **Tell the important people in your life that you're depressed:** Before people can decide to help, they need to know that something is wrong. If you don't tell them, you can't be sure that they know. As addicted people with depression, we can be incredibly self-centered. When we're into being self-centered, we believe that other people should know what's happening to us even if we don't tell them about it. I've found that most people are terrible mind readers. Unless we tell people what we are experiencing they probably won't know.

So, tell your family and friends that you're depressed. At first they may not believe you. It's difficult for other people to see depression as an illness.

It's easy to see it as a bad mood, laziness, or something else that you could just change if you wanted to. They need to understand that the biological basis of your depression is making it difficult for you to feel good, respond normally, and have a normal amount of energy.

If you're a friend or family member, believe what you're being told. If someone is acting depressed for a prolonged period of time, he or she probably is depressed. It doesn't take a rocket scientist to figure it out. In AA, they say that if it walks like a duck, quacks like a duck, and swims like a duck—*it's probably a duck*. We can apply this simple principle to ourselves and those we know or love. If we feel depressed, act depressed, and have difficulty being our normal selves because of it, we're probably depressed.

This is often a difficult realization. It's easier for your friends and family to believe that you're just having a bad day than it is for them to believe that you have a serious mental health problem that could threaten your addiction recovery and your life. Until you see the truth about your own addiction and depression you won't be able to tell anyone else about it. If you don't tell anyone else about it and keep impressing upon them how serious it is, they either won't know what's wrong or won't believe that it's true. If they don't know or don't believe that you're having serious problems with your depression, they won't be willing or able to help you.

2. **Recognize how your depression has affected your family and friends:** Once you recognize your depression, it's important to recognize that your depressive behaviors have hurt others. We all

tend to use self-defeating behaviors when we feel depressed. This is especially true if we're feeling guilty or ashamed because we are depressed. As a result, we can react to our depression with anger and fear and do things that push away the people that we need most.

Start talking with your family and friends about your depression and the self-defeating behaviors that you use to push other people away when you're depressed. Being depressed doesn't give you permission to abuse those you love and care about. It's your responsibility to identify the problems that you create by how you deal with your depression and to make a commitment to work at changing those behaviors.

If you've been depressed for a long time, it's important for you to recognize that your depression has affected your family and friends. Your depression has caused the people you love and care about to change how they think about you, what they tell you, and how they behave when they're around you.

If you have a loved one who is depressed, it's important to be honest with yourself. Their depression has caused them to act differently. In most cases, the depressed person will have let you down, not once, but many times. They may have failed to fulfill their obligations or responsibilities. They may have started acting in ways that you don't like, respect, or admire. In the past you may have thought that these problems were related to *the kind of person they are*. Once you learn about addiction and depression you can begin to see that these behaviors are caused by an untreated illness. The good news is that depression and addiction are both treatable. People can and will get well. They can only do so when all involved recognize the truth about what's going on. This can be difficult. Most of us have heard the saying: *The truth shall set you free!"* What we often haven't heard is the second part of that saying: *But first the truth shall make you miserable!* This is what the truth does. It hurts and then gives you the information that you need to deal responsibly with the problem. Facing the truth hurts and then gives us the ability to become free of the problem.

If a family member or friend is depressed, you need to recognize what is happening, detach, and get as much information as you can. Then it's time for the family and friends to start taking good care of themselves. If you've ever been on an airplane you've heard this announcement: "In the unlikely event that the cabin should depressurize, yellow oxygen masks will appear from the panels above your head. If you are traveling with a child, put your own oxygen mask on first, then assist your child." Why do they want you to take care of yourself first? The answer is really simple: If we don't take care of ourselves first, we won't be able to take care of anyone else. If your friends and family members don't detach from you and start taking care of themselves, they won't be able to effectively support your recovery.

If you have a family member or friend who is depressed and you want to help, it's important to recognize that you will need help and support for yourself. If you don't get the help and support you need, you can easily, and with the best of intentions, become part of the problem instead of part of the solution. You can be drawn into your friend's or family member's depression. This can make you start feeling depressed, angry, and dysfunctional. If you have never attended

Alanon, a Twelve-Step support group for families of alcoholics, this would be a good time to start. Alanon can give the family members and friends of depressed recovering addicts a program of living that will help to detach from friend's or family member's depression and addiction, while continuing to support him or her as a person. In Alanon, this is called *detaching with love*. Detach from the problem by refusing to get sucked into the problem, while refusing to abandon the person. To do this, the friends and family members of depressed people have to learn how to take care of themselves so they can be in a good position to help.

Part 7:
Antidepressant
Medications

7-1. Personal Disclaimer

The use of antidepressant medications is so widespread among recovering people that it's important to discuss it in any book on depression. I want to make two very important disclaimers: First, I'm not a psychiatrist or a medical doctor. I speak from my thirty-five years of experience working with relapse-prone addicts and discussions I've had with many doctors and therapists who treat them. Second, I don't know you or the specific details of the problems you're having with addiction and depression. As a result, there is no way I can give you any specific advice or recommendations except on a very general level. In this section, what I want to do is give you enough general information so you will be able to discuss the issue with your doctor. Let's begin with some basics.

7-2. Biopsychosocial Approach to Depression Management

I strongly believe that to effectively manage depression, a biopsychosocial approach is most effective. Brain chemistry must be stabilized with the use of proper diet, exercise, and appropriate medication. The depressive thought patterns that produce a sense of helplessness and hopelessness must be changed by cognitive therapy, supportive Twelve-Step programs, and reality-testing conversations with trusted friends and other recovering people. The self-defeating behaviors related to the depression must be changed by establishing a schedule of recovery activities that keep us active and appropriately involved in life.

Although medication is helpful and often necessary in the treatment of depression, medication alone doesn't address the psychosocial aspects of depression. As a result, medication alone is often not enough to bring about the full remission of depression. This is because medication alone won't change the content of your thinking, what you are doing, where you go, or how you relate to other people. This requires specific cognitive-behavioral-social therapy for depression.

The best approach to the treatment of depression is to combine antidepressant medication with a program of psychosocial therapy and personal recovery activities designed to specifically address the symptoms of addiction and the related problems that are keeping the depression alive.

7-3. Antidepressant Medications and People Recovering from Addiction

There has recently been a strong focus on the use of antidepressant medications and there is definitely a role for medication in the treatment of addicted people with depressive illness. I have known many chronic relapsers with severe depression who were unable to maintain sobriety because of severe depression. Some of them committed suicide while abstinent from alcohol and other drugs. Others developed a pattern of chronic relapse. Many of these chronic relapsers were able to find long-term recovery when they added the supervised use of antidepressants to their recovery program. In this section, I want to explore a variety of issues involved in the appropriate use of antidepressant medications.

Every day, researchers are learning more about the physical brain processes that influence depression. Based on this research, drug companies are constantly introducing new and more effective antidepressant medications that target specific brain processes involved in depression. Unfortunately, no antidepressant medication is 100-percent effective and there are side effects that can cause problems ranging from nuisances to serious medical problems. As a result, care should be taken in making the decision to use antidepressant medication.

Many professionals and recovering people have mixed feelings about the use of antidepressant medications for people recovering from addiction. In the guide *The A.A. Member—Medications and Other Drugs*, this issue is specifically addressed. Here are a few excerpts:

...A.A. members and many of their physicians have described situations in which depressed patients have been told by A.A.s to throw away the pills, only to have depression return with all its difficulties, sometimes resulting in suicide. We have heard, too, from schizophrenics, manic depressives, epileptics, and others requiring medication that well-meaning A.A. friends often discourage them from taking prescribed medication. Unfortunately, by following a layman's advice, the sufferers find their conditions can return with all their previous intensity....

It becomes clear that just as it is wrong to enable or support any alcoholic to become readdicted to any drug, it's equally wrong to deprive any alcoholic of medication which can alleviate or control other disabling physical and/or emotional problems.—Excerpted from page 13, *The A.A. Member—Medications and Other Drugs*

Medical professionals recognize that psychiatric medications can be an integral part of a recovering person's plan to manage their emotional or psychiatric illness in a healthy and constructive way. However, the medications that some individuals need to take can have the potential for abuse or physical dependence. These medications, when properly prescribed and taken precisely as directed, can be an important tool in controlling psychiatric symptoms and may be crucial to an individual's recovery from their illness and chemical dependency. You need to use caution with your medications and understand that at times, medication is the only option available. Your doctor knows best. As long as you are rigorously honest with your doctor and treatment professionals in regard to your illnesses and history of chemical dependency and use these medications as prescribed, then they will not interfere with your sobriety or recognized clean time. (Hammond and Gorski 2005)

7-4. The Role of Antidepressant Medication in Addiction Treatment

There is definitely a role for antidepressant medications in the treatment of addicted people suffering from depression. The dose and length of time that antidepressants are used will vary depending on a number of factors including the following:

1. The type and severity of the depression;

2. the other forms of therapy and recovery programs that are used with the medication; and

3. the willingness of the person using the medication to make important lifestyle changes that lower stress, improve nutrition, and eliminate stressors that trigger depressive symptoms.

Antidepressant medication can be used to temporarily stabilize brain-chemistry imbalances that cause or perpetuate the feelings of helplessness and hopelessness associated with depression. When used in this way, people are stabilized and maintained on antidepressant medication for a period of about eighteen months while they participate in other forms of treatment and recovery programs designed to increase their ability to avoid and manage depressive symptoms. Research has suggested that people who discontinue their antidepressants before eighteen months are more likely to relapse back into severe depression.

After eighteen months and the development of a stable and effective lifestyle and life management skills, the amount of the antidepressant medication is slowly decreased over a period of twelve to eighteen months. It is important to remember that antidepressants require about four to six weeks to start working. The effects of each reduction in medication will not show up for a period of six to eight weeks. Therefore, the gradual withdrawal from antidepressants should be done with small decreases in dose spaced eight to twelve weeks apart. This routine will give the natural capabilities of the brain time to begin producing endogenous antidepressants.

Medication, however, will do nothing to help clients develop the psychological and social skills needed to develop a feeling of confidence in dealing with life problems. The antidepressant medication will change the underlying brain chemistry. It will not change any situational or lifestyle problems. It also won't change deeply entrenched negative or depressive thinking. Antidepressants don't teach people new emotional, stress, and life-management skills. I recommend viewing antidepressants as a tool for lowering the severity of the symptoms of depression to the point where other forms of therapy and personal-recovery activities can be used to develop new ways of thinking, managing feelings, and behaving when involved in important life activities. As the antidepressants stabilize the symptoms of depression, it is also possible to solve situational problems and to make changes in lifestyle that were impossible when limited by the severe symptoms of depression. These changes are all needed to improve life satisfaction and learn to cope with the stress and problems of life. Here's how I think about it: Antidepressants lower my symptoms so that I am able to work at other areas of my recovery without having my depression interfere.

The use of medication as the only therapeutic intervention can result in three things: (1) a life-long dependency on the medication, (2) rapid relapse back into depression once medication is discontinued, and (3) the perpetuation of life problems and stressors that are disrupting your brain chemistry in a way that contributes to continued symptoms of depression. Antidepressants will make you feel less depressed, but they will do nothing to correct the problems with thinking, managing feelings, managing behavior, and lifestyle management that are subjecting you to the high levels of stress that keep driving the depression.

When medication is used in isolation from other treatments designed to identify and change the psychological and social processes that are elevating your stress and driving your depression, the relief is often temporary. The brain chemistry is temporarily adjusted while the psychological and social processes that drive the depression continue. As a result, there is often a need for more medication or a different type of medication to deal with the symptoms of depression that keep returning. If you don't work a full program of recovery, you will probably find the symptoms of your depression returning within six to eighteen months, requiring an increase or a change in the medication used.

The most effective use of antidepressant medication occurs when the treatment of depression is closely coordinated with the treatment of chemical dependency. In other words, medication for depression is best viewed as an adjunct to a structured addiction recovery program that has been modified to include specific activities and forms of therapy that will support recovery from both addiction and depression.

7-5. Special Problems for Recovering Addicts Using Antidepressants

Antidepressant medications, especially the SSRIs, can cause special problems for chemically dependent patients if used outside the context of a structured recovery program.

Many chemically dependent patients want to use antidepressant medications instead of participating in structured therapy and self-help programs. They want instant relief to emotional distress through medications and have difficulty tolerating the normal cycles of depression and agitation that are part of life and living.

Recovering addicts also believe in *"better living through chemistry."* They are conditioned by their addiction to place magical expectations on the wonderful things that drugs can do for them. They also psychologically empower the medications they use in such a way that they become dependent on any mood-altering substance they tend to use. Once they start using an antidepressant, they expect a magical cure and feel an urge to stop using other recovery tools.

If side effects occur, recovering addicts will often request other medications with a higher addiction potential to manage the side effects. As a result, caution must be used when using antidepressant medications for chemically dependent patients.

It must be remembered, however, that some people will have severe brain-chemistry imbalances that may require the life-long use of antidepressants. Even these individuals, however, will benefit significantly from using therapy and personal recovery activities simultaneously with their medication. In many cases the appropriate use of related therapies can prevent the need for gradually increasing or changing medication over time. At times it can even allow for the effective management of depression while using smaller doses of antidepressant medication.

7-6. Antidepressant Medications as a Substitute for Psychotherapy

The use of antidepressant medications in the treatment of depression has tended to emphasize the use of medications as a substitute for psychotherapy. This trend has been strongly influenced by the pressures of medical cost containment. It is less expensive to treat depression with medication than it is to treat it with psychotherapy. However, the limitations of the use of antidepressant medications as a substitute for psychotherapy have been recognized since the late 1970s.

Aaron Beck (Beck 1979) points out six limitations of using antidepressant medication without concurrent therapy and recovery programs:

1. **Effectiveness of Tricyclic Medication:** 60–65 percent of depressed clients show a definite improvement as a result of treatment with common tricyclic medications (see Beck 1973, pg. 86). This means that 35–40 percent of depressed clients do not improve with tricyclic medications.

2. **Effectiveness of Selective Serotonin Reuptake Inhibitors (SSRIs):** Selective serotonin reuptake inhibitors (such as Prozac, Paxil, etc.) have fewer side effects than tricyclic medications and about the same rate of therapeutic effectiveness (i.e., a 60–65-percent improvement rate and 35–40-percent non-improvement rate).

3. **Refusal and Noncompliance with Medication:** Many depressed clients either refuse or cannot safely use antidepressant medications. These groups include pregnant women, clients with co-occurring substance-use disorders who strongly believe that any mood-altering medication can lead to relapse to their substance-use disorder, those who refuse to take antidepressants for fear of side effects, and those who stop taking them as a result of side effects.

4. **Late Start of Medication:** Many depressed people will not start using antidepressants until their depression has persisted for a long time and becomes very severe. As a result, many psychosocial problems surrounding the depression have already developed and become habituated. Medication alone will not resolve these psychosocial problems.

5. **The Problem of Attribution:** It is possible that in the long run, the reliance on medication might indirectly undermine the patient's utilization of his or her own psychological tools for coping with depression. This is because *many patients who successfully use antidepressant medications will attribute their problem with depression solely to their use of the medication.* I have heard many people say, "Now that I'm on my antidepressants I feel fine. I guess all my life problems were caused by my brain-chemistry imbalances. So I've stopped attending meetings and working a program." Many of these people have significant psychological and social problems beyond their depression, but because the depression is gone, their motivation to look honestly at their life and set up a recovery program to improve their problems disappears.

Other patients tend to attribute the entire reduction of their depression to the medication, even though they have used many other behavioral and cognitive methods and made substantial social changes during the course of using the medication. (Shapiro and Morris 1978)

There is a high relapse rate of patients who have been successfully treated with antidepressant medications and then discontinue the medication. This rate has been estimated to be as high as 50 percent (see Beck 1979, pg. 3). The problem of attribution discussed above could be a significant contributor to relapse because the client fails to develop biopsychosocial skills for the management of depression.

7-7. The Effectiveness of Cognitive Therapy on Depression

The use of cognitive therapy with depression has been proven to be as effective in reducing the severity of depressive symptoms as has the use of antidepressants. There is significant overlap in the types of patients capable of benefiting from either medication or cognitive therapy for depression. These patients would benefit from either form of therapy. There are some patients who benefit from medication who do not respond to cognitive therapy. There are some patients who benefit from cognitive therapy who do not respond well to medications.

The effectiveness of cognitive therapy in the treatment of depression may be related to the following:

1. Learning basic lifestyle management skills (lifestyle restructuring that establishes effective routine habits of daily living that include proper diet, exercise, stress management, relationship management, and conflict resolution skills).

117

2. Learning basic emotional and behavioral management skills including: (a) the skills associated with self-motivation, goal setting, and consistent follow-through; and (b) the skills associated with *impulse control* when applied to the self-defeating urges to isolate, socially withdraw, abandon daily structure and routine, stop setting goals, or stop following through on action steps needed to accomplish important goals.

3. Learning emotional management skills. These basic skills involve the ability to recognize, accurately label, and communicate feelings and emotions in a socially appropriate manner.

4. Learning thinking and problem-solving skills. These basic skills involve learning how to identify inner thoughts and dialogues; distinguish among addictive, depressive, and healthy inner dialogues; and learning how to challenge depressive ways of thinking.

5. Learning relapse prevention skills. This involves learning how to identify and manage high-risk situations, lifestyle problems, and psychosocial responses that previously caused depression.

6. Learning relapse management skills. This involves developing a specific plan for recognizing the early symptoms of depression and taking immediate action to stop the depressive episode quickly.

7. Integrated use of antidepressants and psychotherapy. There is a growing consensus that the most effective use of antidepressant medication is in conjunction with a program of psychotherapy that focuses on the symptoms of depression and addiction as an interrelated network of problems that tend to reinforce each other.

7-8. Positions on the Use of Antidepressants and Addiction Recovery

There appears to be three common positions on the issue of the use of antidepressants by recovering alcoholics and other drug addicts. These can be summarized as: the *anti-medication fundamentalists,* the *pro-medication advocates,* and *medication realists.*

The ***Anti-Medication Fundamentalists*** believe that recovering people should be completely free from all drugs including psychiatric medications like antidepressants. Their position is simple: these medications alter your mood, and the goal of recovery is to learn how to manage your moods without using any medications at all. Some of the really strict anti-medication extremists won't even take aspirin for a toothache.

Pro-Medication Advocates believe that if you are having problems in recovery and there is a non-addictive medication that can help, you should try it. Many of these pro-medication advocates use antidepressants themselves and have had good experiences. They found them to be helpful with no significant side effects or problems.

The ***Medication Conservatives*** believe that antidepressants should be used if the depression is interfering with addiction recovery or the normal activities of life, but great care should be taken to protect against becoming addicted to the medication.

7-9 Conservative Guiding Principles

People I know who are conservative about the use of antidepressants but do believe these medications should be used when needed tend to follow these guiding principles:

119

1.   There are two goals of addiction recovery: total abstinence from alcohol and other mind-altering drugs plus the ability to live a meaningful and effective life.

2.   There are special circumstances that require the responsible use of medication. These special circumstances can include but are not limited to surgery and post-surgical recovery, injuries or conditions causing severe immediate (acute) pain, long-term (chronic) pain disorders, and psychiatric illnesses with symptoms that are so severe they are interfering with addiction recovery, increasing the risk of relapse, or interfering with the ability to live a meaningful and functional life. These psychiatric illnesses can include depression, mania or manic depression, and psychosis.

3.   When possible, other treatments that don't involve the use of mind-altering medications should be used first to try and manage the symptoms.

4.   If these nonmedical methods fail, medication can be considered.

5.   If medication is used, medication should always be used cautiously and conservatively.

6.   All medications should always be carefully monitored by a doctor who understands addiction and should accompany a program of cognitive therapy to help reduce depressive thinking.

7.   Medication should be used for the period of time needed to achieve and maintain the therapeutic effect. (Medication conservatives do recognize that certain severe and persistent illnesses such as depression and schizophrenia may require life-long management.)

8.   Special precautions should be taken against becoming dependent on or addicted to the new medi-

cation or causing a relapse back into addiction to the primary drug of choice. The doctor who is prescribing the medication and other members of the treatment team should watch closely for drug-seeking behavior or the attempt to manipulate other mood-altering drugs from the doctor.

Some doctors are **Pro-Medication Liberals**. They have a reputation in the community for being very loose with a prescription pad. They readily prescribe mood-altering medications to their patients even if they know the patient is in recovery from addiction. They often lack an accurate and detailed understanding of addiction and believe the medications they are prescribing can be helpful. They are easily manipulated by actively addicted people into prescribing pain killers, sedatives, sleeping pills, and other medications that have pleasant mood-altering effects. *People in recovery from addiction should avoid doctors who are pro-medication liberals.* Because these doctors don't recognize the risk these medications can pose to recovering people, they often prescribe medications that reactivate the addiction.

7-10. Types of Antidepressant Medication

There are a number of medications that have proven helpful in the management of depression. We will look at the major antidepressants by dividing them into the following categories:

1.   Tricyclic antidepressants: Elavil, Tofranil, Pamelor, Sinoquan, Norpramin, and Anafranil.

2.   Monoamine oxidase (MAO) inhibitors.

3.   Selective serotonin reuptake inhibitors (SSRIs) are the antidepressants such as Prozac, Zoloft, Paxil, Luvox, Celexa, and Effexor. These SSRIs are

antidepressant medications that affect the neu-rotransmitter serotonin. Newer antidepressants also affect the levels of dopamine, or norepinephrine. SS-RIs generally have fewer side effects than tricyclics.

4. Other prescription antidepressants: Well-butrin, Serzone, and Remeron.

5. Over-the-counter antidepressants: SAM-e and St. John's Wort.

Antidepressants require careful medical management

Antidepressants require careful medical manage-ment. Although many family physicians prescribe and monitor the use of antidepressants, it is a good idea to consult with a psychiatrist who has knowl-edge and experience in treating addicted people suffering from depression. This is especially true if the depression is severe, accompanied by suicidal thoughts or attempts, or is seriously interfering with the ability to function. Antidepressants need to be medically managed because not all people respond to antidepressants in the same way. For them to be effective, your doctor may need to gradually increase the dosage of the prescribed antidepressant or try a variety of different antidepressants to find the one that works for you. Your doctor may even need to pre-scribe two or more antidepressants in combination in order for them to relieve your depressive symptoms. Although some improvements may be seen in the first few weeks, antidepressant medications must be taken regularly for at least three to four weeks (in some cases, as many as eight weeks) before the full therapeutic effect occurs.

Patients are often tempted to stop medication too soon. They may feel better and think they no longer need it. Or they may think the medication isn't helping at all because they haven't been taking it long enough for the full therapeutic effect to be felt. It is important to keep taking medication until it has a chance to work. Once you start feeling better, it's important to continue the medication for at least twelve to eighteen months to prevent a recurrence of the depression.

If you decide to stop using the medication, it is important that this decision be discussed with the entire treatment team, including your psychiatrist, the therapist helping you with the psychosocial aspects of your recovery from depression, and the addiction professionals who are monitoring your addiction recovery.

If you do decide to stop, remember that *some medications (including most of the SSRIs) must be stopped gradually to give the body time to adjust. Never stop taking an antidepressant without consulting the doctor for instructions on how to safely discontinue the medication.* For individuals with bipolar disorder or chronic major depression, medication may have to be maintained indefinitely.

Antidepressant drugs are not habit-forming. However, as is the case with any type of medication prescribed for more than a few days, antidepressants have to be carefully monitored to see if the correct dosage is being given. The doctor will check the dosage and its effectiveness regularly.

Medications of any kind—prescribed, over-the-counter, or borrowed—*should never be mixed without consulting the doctor.* Other health professionals who may prescribe a drug—such as a dentist or other medical specialist—should be told of the medications you're taking. Some drugs, although safe when taken alone can, if taken with other medications, cause severe and dangerous side effects. Some drugs, like alcohol or street drugs, may reduce the effectiveness of antidepressants and should be avoided. This includes wine, beer, and hard liquor. Some people who have not had a problem with alcohol use may be permitted by their doctor to use a modest amount of alcohol while taking one of the newer antidepressants. I personally don't believe that this is a good recommendation. If you are in recovery from addiction to alcohol or other drugs, the use of alcohol in any quantity will probably start a progressive relapse process.

Anti-anxiety drugs or sedatives are not antidepressants. They are sometimes prescribed along with antidepressants; however, they are not effective when taken alone for a depressive disorder. Stimulants, such as amphetamines, are not effective antidepressants, but they are used occasionally under close supervision in medically ill depressed patients. Both anti-anxiety medications and amphetamines should be avoided by people in recovery from addiction. These medications have the power to activate craving and usually start the relapse process going full-steam ahead.

Questions about any antidepressant medication prescribed, or problems that may be related to the medication, should be discussed with your doctor and other members of the treatment team who are helping you to recover from both depression and addiction.

Lithium has for many years been the treatment of choice for bipolar disorder. This is because it can be effective in smoothing out the mood swings common to this disorder. Its use must be carefully monitored, as the range between an effective dose and a toxic one is small. If a person has preexisting thyroid, kidney, or heart disorders or epilepsy, lithium may not be recommended. Fortunately, other medications have been found to be of benefit in controlling mood swings. Among these are two mood-stabilizing anticonvulsants: carbamazepine (Tegretol®) and valproate (Depakote®). Both of these medications have gained wide acceptance in clinical practice, and valproate has been approved by the U.S. Food and Drug Administration for first-line treatment of acute mania. Other anticonvulsants that are being used now include lamotrigine (Lamictal®) and gabapentin (Neurontin®): their role in the treatment hierarchy of bipolar disorder remains under study. Treat these medications with the utmost respect and only use them under the strict supervision of a physician who knows your entire history with addiction and depression.

Most people who have bipolar disorder take more than one medication including, along with lithium and/or an anticonvulsant, a medication for accompanying agitation, anxiety, depression, or insomnia. Finding the best possible combination of these medications is of importance to the patient and requires close monitoring by the physician.

7-11. Side Effects of Antidepressant Medication

Antidepressants may cause mild and, usually, temporary side effects (sometimes referred to as adverse effects). Typically these are annoying, but not serious. However, some people do experience serious and even life-threatening side effects. Although they are rare, it's important to be aware of them. Any unusual reactions or side effects that interfere with functioning should be reported to the doctor immediately. Appendix 9 contains a more detailed list of possible side effects that can help you evaluate problems and accurately report them to your doctor and treatment team.

7-12. Addiction Potential of Antidepressant Medication

Addiction or biopsychosocial dependence is marked by a pattern of compulsive drug use. Most authorities do not regard antidepressants as causing addiction but this has been challenged. This debate is inconclusive but needs to be discussed with your physician when considering antidepressant medication.

Withdrawal or discontinuation symptoms have been recognized with antidepressants, but other features of addiction related to patterns of compulsive use and craving the immediate mood-altering effects of antidepressants have not appeared. The absence of acute "desirable" effects make addiction theoretically unlikely, although problems with physical dependence are causing most doctors to recommend that patients who want to stop the antidepressants do so slowly over a long period of time.

Two antidepressants do have a tendency to cause addiction. These are tranylcypromine (Parnate®)and amineptine (Survector®) and should be avoided in those with a history of substance abuse. Patients prescribed other antidepressants should be told that they are not addictive. (Moorside 1999)

126

7-13. Herbal Remedies

In the past few years, much interest has arisen in the use of herbs in the treatment of both depression and anxiety. *St. John's Wort* (*Hypericum perforatum*), an herb used extensively in the treatment of mild to moderate depression in Europe, has recently aroused interest in the United States. Although many people strongly believe in the effectiveness of these medications, the scientific studies have been inconclusive.

The Food and Drug Administration issued a *Public Health Advisory* on February 10, 2000, which states that St. John's Wort appears to affect an important metabolic pathway that is used by many drugs prescribed to treat conditions such as AIDS, heart disease, depression, seizures, certain cancers, and rejection of transplants. Therefore, health-care providers should alert their patients about these potential drug interactions.

Some other herbal supplements frequently used that have not been evaluated in large-scale clinical trials are gingko biloba, echinacea, and ginseng. Any herbal supplement should be taken only after consultation with the doctor or other health-care provider.

7-14. Psychotherapy

Many forms of psychotherapy, including some short-term (ten to twenty week) therapies, can help depressed individuals. "Talking" therapies help patients gain insight into and resolve their problems through verbal exchange with the therapist, sometimes combined with "homework" assignments between sessions. "Behavioral" therapists help patients learn how to obtain more satisfaction and rewards through their own actions and how to unlearn the behavioral patterns that contribute to or result from their depression.

Two of the short-term psychotherapies that research has shown helpful for some forms of depression are interpersonal and cognitive/behavioral therapies. Interpersonal therapists focus on the patient's disturbed personal relationships that both cause and exacerbate (or increase) the depression. Cognitive/behavioral therapists help patients change the negative styles of thinking and behaving often associated with depression.

Psychodynamic therapies, which are sometimes used to treat depressed persons, focus on resolving the patient's conflicted feelings. These therapies are often reserved until the depressive symptoms are significantly improved. In general, severe depressive illnesses, particularly those that are recurrent, will require medication (or electroconvulsive therapy [ECT] under special conditions) along with, or preceding, psychotherapy for the best outcome.

Although it is possible to recover from depression, there is no one correct way to do it. Different people use different recovery tools. What works well for one person may not work very well for another. Yet there are general principles and basic tools that are effective for a large number of people. This means that putting together a recovery program from addiction and depression will require learning about the choices that are available to you. It means being willing to put together an initial recovery plan and being open to adjust the details of that plan in order to make it work more effectively. In recovery, *we seek progress not perfection*. We take small steps that make us feel a little bit better. We learn from those steps, and then take other small steps.

Part 8: Depression Management Toolkit

> *No matter how bad I feel today I will remember that I am more than my depression.*
> *I am a conscious being capable of rising above my depression.*

We have the ability to rise above our depression and manage it more effectively. I know it usually doesn't seem that way. It's easy to get trapped by the mistaken beliefs of depression. These depressive beliefs tell us we're powerless, it's hopeless, and nothing can be done to change it. Fortunately, these mistaken beliefs are just that—mistaken. These beliefs make sense given how bad we are feeling, the circumstances we are in, and the limited information we have about depression and recovery. With new knowledge comes a new understanding that can open the doors of recovery and more helpful beliefs.

> **It's easy to get trapped in the mistaken beliefs of depression that tell us we're powerless, it's hopeless, and nothing can be done. Fortunately, these mistaken beliefs are just that—mistaken.**

I can tell you with absolute certainty that the beliefs that keep us trapped in depression are false beliefs. The following tool kit provides a wide variety of things we can do to manage our depression and start feeling a little better. These tools are helpful, but you have to make a conscious decision to use them on a daily basis. These tools won't *cure* your depression, but they will help you feel at least a little bit better every time you use them. Over time, as you develop the skill of using the tools correctly, you will be able to manage your depression more effectively and have longer periods of time when you are able to live without feeling depressed.

The best way to use this toolkit is to read the list of tools quickly and then select two or three of the tools you believe might work for you. Then read the description of these tools again and develop a written plan for putting them to work in your life. Let's review these tools.

Tool #1: Keep a Recovery Journal

Using a recovery journal to write to yourself and monitor your moods is an excellent way to unburden yourself. Write not only about things that are troubling you or that you are struggling with, but the things you find that work to lift your depression. For example, write for fifteen to twenty minutes a day and keep it up for several days. First express your feelings, then weave a narrative. Reread your journal and try to find some meaning in the problems that you are recording. We often have solutions that we discount or don't fully develop.

Tool #2: Be Honest with Yourself about Your Depression

The first step in managing depression is to be honest about the fact that you're depressed. This means admitting that you're depressed and figuring out how serious your depression is. It also means evaluating how your depression is affecting the people and things in your life that you value most.

Depression is a serious illness and can lead to lost jobs, lost friends, lost families, suicide attempts, and death. It's easy to deny or minimize the seriousness of our depression. When we can convince ourselves that it's not that bad, we can tell ourselves we don't need to do anything about it. When we don't do anything about it, our depression usually keeps getting worse.

You can evaluate your depression by completing a depression symptom check list (see Appendix 1) and learning how to self-monitor your depression. Self-monitoring means *consciously noticing the symptoms of your depression, when they occur, and what's happening around you when they occur.*

When you notice that you're feeling depressed, don't run away from it. Face the depression. Look it right in the eye and see exactly how bad the symptoms are in the moment. Don't turn away and pretend it's not there. Don't run from it. The first step in dealing with any problem is to face it. So when you feel depressed, acknowledge it. Say something like this to yourself: *"Right now I'm feeling depressed."*

The first step in dealing with any problem is to face it.

Don't waste your time trying to figure out why you're depressed, because that will come later. Early in your recovery from depression, asking why you're depressed will usually just make you more depressed. Focus instead on describing the symptoms of your depression as accurately as you can and doing things that can make you feel a little bit better right now. There will be plenty of time later in your recovery to identify the other problems that are related to your depression. Right now, your number-one problem is to recognize your depression and manage the immediate symptoms so that you can feel better, function better, avoid using alcohol or other drugs for relief, and avoid drastic problems like losing your family, your job, or even your life.

Focus on:
1. Describing the symptoms of your depression as accurately as you can.
2. Doing things that can make you feel a little bit better right now.

Here are some things that you can ask yourself to determine how severe your depression is:

Depression Severity Questionnaire

1. Am I feeling depressed right now?
   ❏ Yes ❏ No ❏ Unsure

2. How bad is my depression right now (i.e., how severe are the symptoms?)? You can rate the current severity of your depression by selecting one of the following statements:

Right now my depression is *a nuisance*: I am able to function normally despite my depression by using extra effort to focus on what I want to do and forcing myself to go through the steps of getting it done. (This is mild depression that is rated between 1 and 3 on a ten-point scale. You can write this in your recovery journal like this: "Right now I rate the severity of my depression as <select a number 1–3>.")

Right now my depression is *an interference*: My depression is draining so much of my energy that sometimes I can't be sure I can function normally even when I use extra effort. Not knowing if I'll be able to function or not causes me anxiety, guilt, and shame. When I can't do what I need to do it causes real problems in my life. (This is moderate depression that is rated between 4 and 6 on a ten-point scale. You can write this in your recovery journal like this: "Right now I rate the severity of my depression as <select a number 4–6>.")

Right now my depression is *a disability*: My depression is so severe that I can't force myself to function normally no matter what I do. (This is severe depression that is rated between 7 and 9 on a ten-point scale. You can write this in your recovery journal like this: "Right now I rate the severity of my depression as <select a number between 7–9>.")

Right now my depression *a suicidal threat*:
My depression is causing me so much pain and I'm so
tired of living with that pain that I'm thinking about
killing myself. (This is life-threatening depression
that is rated as a 10 on a ten-point scale. You can
write this in your recovery journal like this: "Right
now I rate the severity of my depression as <select
the number 10>.")

Below is a simple severity scale that you can use to
evaluate your current level of depression. This severity scale will allow you to see in a graphic way exactly
how depressed you are. This will give you the ability
to determine how much time, effort, and resources
you need to put into your recovery. Just take the nu-
merical answers from the above questions and circle
the numbers on The Depression Severity Scale.

Depression Severity Scale

1 —— 2 —— 3 —— 4 —— 5 —— 6 —— 7 —— 8 —— 9 —— 10

Nuisance   Interference   Disability   Suicidal Threat

**Tool #3: Make the Commitment to Get Started
Immediately**

The second step in recovering from depression is
to get started. It may seem like an impossible task at
first but it's not. There are literally thousands of people around the United States who have successfully
recovered from serious depression and are living a
meaningful and comfortable life. If you calmly start
using the tools described in this book, you'll be on
your way to recovering from depression and it won't
be nearly as bad as you thought it would be.

If you scored above seven on the *Depression Severity Questionnaire* (the questionnaire that you just completed above) you need to get help immediately. There are two steps to getting help: (1) Tell a family member or close friend about your depression and your decision to get help. (2) Ask them to support you in getting help. Ask them to hold you accountable for following through. If you don't ask for help and make yourself accountable to someone other than yourself, your chances of following through are not good. Without the help and support of another person you could easily lapse back into a depressive episode and forget about your commitment.

As a child, I became fascinated by the back of a box of Borax bleach. First I noticed the twenty-mule team pulling a heavily loaded wagon through the desert. Then I read this inscription written artfully beneath the picture:

> **There are many bleached bones on the battlefield of decision.**
>
> **For at the moment of choice, we can pause and die in the waiting.**

I've worked with many people who have been seriously depressed for years. Their depression crept up on them an inch at a time. They slowly adjusted their lives to accommodate it. They trained the people around them to accommodate their depression and leave them alone. By the time I saw them, many were at risk of relapsing to alcohol or drug use or committing suicide in sobriety. Many of these severely depressed people refused to acknowledge they were depressed. Others admitted they were depressed but refused to admit they needed a different set of tools to manage their depression than they used to manage their sobriety.

The tragedy is this: All of these people could have decided years before that they were depressed and sought help to manage it. Most didn't because they lacked the information and support they needed to get help.

Now it's time for you to decide. This decision will affect you and those you love. It will either set you on a path to recovery from depression, or it will keep you trapped in the depression cycle. We don't have to do anything special to stay trapped in depression. All we have to do is refuse to make the decision to start a recovery program that makes depression one of our top priorities. Here are some questions to think about.

**We don't have to do any special
to stay trapped in depression.
All we have to do is
refuse to make the decision
to start a recovery program.**

---

1.   Am I willing to keep living with my current level of depression?

2.   How much time, energy, and resources am I willing to lose because I refuse to declare war on my depression and decide to recover? (Remember, our depression is an expensive habit that costs us time, money, relationships, jobs, and quality of life.)

3.   Am I willing to make learning how to manage my depression my number-one priority?

If the answer is, *"NO, I'm not willing to keep living with it! YES, I'm willing to make depression management a top priority in my life,"* you're ready to go to the next step. Remember, half measures avail us nothing. You are now at a critical turning point in making a genuine commitment to learn how to manage your depression more effectively. The decision is yours!

Tool #4: Declare War against Your Depression

Declaring war means three things: First, making the management of depression your top priority; second, grieving the losses caused by depression; and third, giving up the right to use depression as an excuse for refusing to do what you need to do to manage your depression more effectively.

Unfortunately, many of us mistakenly believe we can't do anything to manage our depression until we start feeling less depressed. To tell yourself, "I'll start a recovery program as soon as I start feeling better!" is almost as silly as saying "I'm too sick to go to the hospital."

We need to start a recovery program when we're feeling our worst. This is how we start to feel better. We must do things now in order to feel less depressed later on. In other words, we must force ourselves to start using depression management tools while we're still feeling depressed. Here's how you can do it.

We need to start a recovery program when we're feeling our worst. We must do things now in order to feel less depressed later on.

---

1. **Make Managing Depression Your Number-One Priority:** Make a commitment to yourself, to another human being, and to the God of your understanding that you will do everything in your power to learn about and manage your depression.

2. **Use Anger as a Motivational Tool to Get Started:** Allow yourself to get angry at your depression and what it has done to you.

If your depression were a person who was causing you the level of pain and problems that you are currently experiencing as a result of your depression, what would you say to that person? Think of all of the pain and problems you have experienced because of your depression. Imagine that your depression is a living, breathing entity whose purpose is to slowly steal your energy, your will to live, and eventually your life itself. Imagine that your depression is an entity that steals your ability to enjoy anyone or anything of value in your life. Imagine your depression is stealing your self-confidence and self-worth. Your depression wants you to feel helpless, hopeless, and powerless so it can keep victimizing you. Your depression wants you to give away your power by believing that you are useless and incompetent and there is nothing you can do to get better.

How do you feel about that? Connect with your anger and direct that energy into learning recovery skills.

3. **Grieve Your Losses:** Allow yourself to feel sad about the losses you have experienced that are related to your depression.

Some of us experience a serious loss that activates our depression. At other times our depression causes us to become so dysfunctional that we lose friends, family, relationships, jobs, and many meaningful life experiences. Most depressed people experience both types of loss. It's OK to feel the pain, talk about it with others, and grieve the loss.

4. **Make the Choice to Recover:** Don't upset yourself with the fact that you are feeling depressed. Say to yourself, *"I am feeling depressed, but I have a choice. I can choose to do things that will make my depression a little bit better or I can choose to do things to make my depression a little bit worse. If I refuse to make the choice, my depression will make it for me. Do I want my depression to control me and destroy my life, or do I choose to start doing things to make my depression a little bit better?"*

Tool #5: Schedule of Daily Activities (Recovery Program)

Having unstructured time can be the kiss of death for people with a tendency toward depression. The best way to manage the depression is to keep busy. Because our depression will rob us of energy and make us lose our desire to do anything except sit around, we need to schedule activities each day and ask other people to work with us to encourage us to participate in those activities.

A typical daily schedule will involve a set time to get up in the morning, a set time to go to bed at night, and a routine schedule of activities that we get into the habit of doing each day. Make the schedule simple and easy to follow. A typical schedule might look like this:

6:30 a.m.:   Get up, read my daily meditation, shower, shave, get dressed, and have a light breakfast.

7:30 a.m.:	Leave for work. (It usually takes 15 minutes to get there but I'll get in the habit of giving myself plenty of time to avoid problems.)
8:00 a.m.:	Arrive at work and start my morning schedule.
10:00 a.m.:	Take a fifteen-minute break, have a nutritious snack, and take a short walk.
10:15 a.m.:	Back to work and complete the morning work schedule.
12:00 noon:	Take a lunch break, eat a light but nutritious lunch, call my sponsor or a support person to check in.
1:00 p.m.:	Back to work and start my afternoon work schedule.
2:30 p.m.:	Take a fifteen-minute break, have a snack, take a short walk.
2:45 p.m.:	Back to work and complete the afternoon work schedule.
4:00 p.m.:	Leave work, go home to change clothes and have dinner.
7:30 p.m.:	Leave for my 8:00 p.m. Twelve-Step meeting.
8:30 p.m.:	Have coffee with my sponsor.
9:30 p.m.:	Head for home to spend a little time with my spouse.
10:30 p.m.:	Wind down and go to bed.

Tool #6: Get Evaluated for Antidepressant Medication

Get a physical examination and honestly discuss your depression with your physician. If you are in recovery from addiction or another mental health problem, see the same doctor who is currently managing your recovery and talk with your therapist and other members of your treatment team. Your physician or counselor can conduct an evaluation to screen you for depression.

Your physician may prescribe and manage antidepressant medication or may refer you to a psychiatrist for medication management. Your doctor may also refer you to a therapist (usually a psychologist, social worker, or licensed professional counselor with special training in the treatment of depression). If your doctor doesn't refer you to psychotherapy for depression, it's important to ask for a referral. Psychotherapy can be helpful in reducing the symptoms of depression and solving problems related to the depression that can lead to relapse.

The treatment of choice will depend on the outcome of the evaluation. There are a variety of antidepressant medications and psychotherapies that can be used to treat depressive disorders. Some people with milder forms of depression may do well with psychotherapy alone. People with moderate to severe depression most often benefit from antidepressants. Most will do best with combined treatment: medication to gain relief from severe symptoms and psychotherapy to learn more effective ways to deal with life's problems that can make your depression worse.

Depending on the diagnosis and severity of symptoms, the doctor may prescribe medication and/or one of the several forms of psychotherapy that have proven effective for depression.

Read the section on antidepressant medications (Part 6 of this book, p. 89) before seeing your doctor. Identify any areas you don't understand and bring the book with you to get those questions answered by your doctor. Remember, your depression may not be serious enough to require medication, but it is always good to be working with a doctor if depression is becoming a problem.

Tool #7: Don't Drink or Use Other Substances of Abuse:

Drinking and using other drugs will always make your depression worse, not better. The only exception is the properly managed use of antidepressants as part of your recovery plan. Abstinence from alcohol and other drugs is the foundation for all of the recovery tools that follow.

Fortunately, the recovery plans for addiction and depression are closely related. Many of the things that help people stay comfortably sober also help them manage their depression. This means that a recovery plan that meets the needs of both addiction and depression can be developed. If you're already in recovery from addiction, this is good news. You already know and have practiced many of the recovery skills needed to manage depression. All you will need to do is learn a few additional techniques.

Tool #8: Learn to Manage Suicidal Thoughts

Suicidal thinking is often part of depression. When we start feeling so bad that we believe we can't handle it, death can appear to be the only way out.

So, let's see if having suicidal thoughts is a part of your depression. If you are suicidal, don't get overwhelmed, the last part of this section explains how to manage suicidal thoughts. Let's get started.

Here is a short questionnaire that can help you evaluate if you have suicidal thoughts and how serious they are. (There is another longer questionnaire, *The Suicidal Thoughts Questionnaire—Long Form*, in Appendix 2. Feel free to answer the questions on the long form and bring it with you to your psychiatrist or therapist to detail information about your depression.)

Read each statement below and check the box in front of the answer that fits you best. Notice if thinking about or talking about any of these questions causes you to feel more depressed, get upset, or experience an inner conflict. If you experience an inner conflict, notice there are two sides of your personality fighting with each other—your *Depressed Self* and your *Hopeful Self*. We're going to show you how your *Hopeful Self* can win. (This questionnaire is also reproduced in *Appendix 2: Suicidal Thoughts Questionnaire—Short Form*.)

1. I sometimes feel life isn't worth living.
   ❑ Yes   ❑ No   ❑ Unsure

2. I sometimes think I would be better off dead.
   ❑ Yes   ❑ No   ❑ Unsure

3. I sometimes think about killing myself.
   ❑ Yes   ❑ No   ❑ Unsure

4. I sometimes think about ways of killing myself.
   ❑ Yes   ❑ No   ❑ Unsure

5. I have developed a plan to kill myself.
   ❏ Yes   ❏ No   ❏ Unsure

6. I have everything I need to carry out the plan.
   ❏ Yes   ❏ No   ❏ Unsure

7. I have tried to kill myself in the past.
   ❏ Yes   ❏ No   ❏ Unsure

8. I will probably try to kill myself sometime in the future.
   ❏ Yes   ❏ No   ❏ Unsure

9. I have strong and compelling reasons for staying alive that will keep me from trying to hurt myself.
   ❏ Yes   ❏ No   ❏ Unsure

Note: If you answer "yes" to questions 3, 4, 5, 6, or 8, you are so seriously depressed that you need to seek professional help immediately.

It's also important to talk with your family and friends about your depression and thoughts of suicide. Sit down with them when you have time for a serious discussion and review the questions with them. Share your answers to the questions with them and have an honest talk. Most family members and friends will want to know if you're seriously depressed and need help. Have the courage to reach out and talk to those you love.

If you rated your depression as a seven or above, it's important to get professional help as soon as you can. Take it seriously. No matter how bad your depression is, you can start recovering and feeling better. The longer you wait, however, the more severe your depression may become. If your depression is severe or if you are having thoughts of suicide, call a therapist, a crisis line, or go to the emergency of room of a hospital. (*Check out the Resources Available in Appendix 4.*)

Read this affirmation to yourself and believe what it says, because it's true:

An Affirmation to Fight Depression

Whether I feel like it or not I am an important person.

My life has a meaning and purpose.

There are other people who love and care about me. There are people I love and care about.

It may not *feel* that way in this moment, but it's true.

As I learn to manage my depression, my sense of love, meaning, and purpose will come back.

This period of pain and depression is only temporary. It will pass.

Tool #9: Learn to Detach from Your Depression

Have you ever had a bad cold but had to keep working despite how bad you felt? Most of us have. We keep going by detaching from how bad we feel, rising above the bad feelings, and using our higher self to motivate us to keep going even though we feel sick. This is called detachment.

When we detach from our depression, we don't make our depression go away. We make a decision to rise above our depression and do what we need to do despite the fact that we feel depressed.

In the movie, *Lawrence of Arabia*, Lawrence is with a group of soldiers who are playing a game. They all put money in a pot. Then they each light a match and hold the match in their fingers. The last one to keep holding the match wins all the money.

One by one the soldiers dropped the matches as they burned their fingers. Lawrence held onto the match until it burned out on his finger-tips.

As Lawrence collected his money, one of the soldiers asked him: "What's the trick? How did you keep the match from burning your fingers?"

"There's no trick to keep it from burning your fingers," said Lawrence. "The trick is not to care that your fingers are burning."

In AA this is called *acting as if*. If we want to recover from depression, sometimes we have to do things despite the fact we're really depressed. We have to act as if we're feeling OK when we're not. If we do the right things, we turn down our depressive brain chemistry and start feeling a little bit better. It's important to remember that we must learn how to think better and act better *before* we start feeling better. This means forcing ourselves to change our thoughts and behaviors *especially* when we're feeling depressed.

Here are some simple steps that can help you start learning how to detach. Remember, detachment is a practice that is a lot like meditation. You have to practice it every day in order to build sufficient skill to make it work.

146

Step 1: Separate Yourself from Your Depression: Recognize that your depression operates as if it was a different person who takes over your brain and body. Neuroscientists say that habitual depressive thinking actually creates neurocircuits in the brain. When these circuits are activated, they hijack the brain and push us into automatic depressive thoughts, feelings, and behaviors. These behaviors are not us. They are things we think, feel, and do as a result of the combination of faulty brain chemistry and past learning experiences.

Step 2: Learn How to Detach from Your Depression: Reflecting on the following meditation might help: *I am capable of feeling depressed, but I am not my depression. I am the person who experiences the depression. Therefore I can detach from and release the feelings of depression and still be me.* Relax yourself and say this to yourself three to five times.

Here is another good affirmation to use: *I may be feeling depressed, but I am not my depression. I am the spiritual being who knows that I am depressed. I am the spiritual being who can choose to take action to make the depression a little bit better.*

Step 3: Label Your Depression as a Disorder: Your depression is an illness, disease, or disorder. Your depression is caused by an abnormal brain response to stress combined with automatic thoughts, feelings, and behaviors that make your depression worse. You can learn to function better despite these faulty brain circuits that periodically go off in your brain. You can adjust your life in a way that will allow you to manage your depression while having a meaningful and comfortable life.

Step 4: Tell Yourself Recovery Is Possible: You need to forcefully remind yourself that recovery is possible. Getting better will take time, but if you begin to consistently use the tools that you are learning, you will develop new skills for managing your depression. As a result, the frequency, duration, and severity of your episodes of depression will decrease. In other words, your episodes of depression will occur less often, and when they do occur they will be shorter and cause less severe problems.

Step 5: Change Your Focus: Remind yourself that you can choose to stay preoccupied with your depression or you can choose to force yourself to refocus on learning depression-management skills. If you stay preoccupied with your depression, the symptoms will get worse. If you refocus on recovery skills, you will decrease or completely turn off the feeling of depression and learn skills for preventing or managing future episodes of depression.

Step 6: Distract Yourself from Your Symptoms: Sometimes, when the symptoms of depression get really bad, the best thing to do is to distract yourself by getting intensely involved in something that really interests you in a positive way. This could be recreational such as watching movies or a DVD series. It could be music or books, or getting involved in writing and journaling. It could mean going to a meeting, not to talk about yourself but to listen, and I mean really listen to what other people are saying and try to get out of yourself emotionally.

Most severe episodes of depression are time limited. It's important to develop ways to wait out these time-limited periods of severe symptoms. The best techniques are based on distraction. When you distract yourself, you focus your mind on something else, hopefully something positive. Many people find that listening to music, taking walks, jogging, or swimming are good distractions.

It's helpful to remind yourself that the peak intensity of the symptoms are time limited. Unless you start doing things like ruminating and catastrophizing, the symptoms will usually reach peak intensity and start to decline over a period of thirty to forty-five minutes. In AA, people are taught to use the slogan, *"This, too, shall pass."* The truth is, it always does unless you start doing things that make the symptoms worse.

While waiting out an episode of severe symptoms, remember there is no substitute for being around people who are supportive and will help you get through it.

Remember the story of *Lawrence of Arabia.* As the match burned out against his fingers, he felt excruciating pain, but he didn't care. He maintained his power over the pain and knew it would pass.

This is a difficult concept to grasp. It is possible to be depressed without turning our power over to the depression. Once we know that our depression is caused by a faulty brain circuit reacting to real-life problems, we don't have to be afraid of the depression. It's just depression. It's uncomfortable, inconvenient, and painful. It's not awful, terrible, and unbearable. We can be depressed and learn how to live normally despite the depression. Then we can begin to change how we live by making small choices every day that will help us develop skills we can use to make the depression a little bit better.

Tool #10: Realize You Can Make Things a Little Bit Better

Tell yourself you can choose to do things to make your depression a little bit better. You can also choose to do things that make things a little bit worse. The choice is up to you.

Here's the problem: If you're depressed, you must start thinking and acting better *before* you can start feeling better. In other words, you must make a decision to do things that will help you feel better even though you're feeling depressed. You must stop giving your depression the power to control your life. You must learn that just because you feel depressed doesn't mean that you can't do anything. You can choose to do things that will make you feel a little bit better even though you don't feel like it and even though you don't want to do it.

What are some of these things? Well, it's different for everyone, but here are some ideas.

Thoughts you can think to make yourself feel a little bit better.	Things you can do to make yourself feel a little bit better.
1. I don't have to let depression run my life.	1. Take a walk.
2. Feeling depressed doesn't mean there is nothing good going on in my life. There are good things happening even though I'm feeling depressed. (At this point read your gratitude list.)	2. Talk to a friend.

3. My depression is caused by a faulty brain circuit firing off in my head. I am not going to let a faulty brain circuit control me and what I do.	3. Go to a Twelve-Step meeting.
4. I can do little things despite the fact that I'm feeling depressed (such as taking a bath, taking a walk, going for a swim, etc.).	4. Read your gratitude list.
5. I don't have to believe the addictive thoughts in my head. I can challenge each one as soon as it comes into my head.	5. Remind yourself over and over again that "this, too, shall pass."
6. I don't have to accept the thoughts that say I'm no good or that I'm a loser. I can challenge them as soon as they come into my mind.	6. Take a shower or a bath.
7. Being depressed is a waste of time. As soon as I get serious about focusing on something else that is productive, my depression will lessen.	7. Go for a drive.
8. What are the pleasurable activities that usually make me feel better? (Refer to your *Pleasurable Activities List*.)	8. Say some prayers.

9. Being depressed doesn't necessarily mean that something is going wrong in my life. I'll think it through and make a list of the things that are going well and the things that are going poorly in my life.	9. Clear your mind and meditate.
10. Call a friend and ask for encouragement.	10. Listen to music that you find relaxing and pleasant.

Tool #11: Make a Gratitude List

A *Gratitude List* is a tool that directs and challenges our belief that nothing is going right in our lives. The truth is no matter how bad our lives are, there is always something that is going right. Victor Frankl, a survivor of the Nazi concentration camps, described in his book *Man's Search for Meaning* how the prisoners survived and managed to stay alive and fight against the horrors, abuse, and deprivations of the camps. Dr. Frankl stated that he could predict, with a high degree of accuracy, who would die quickly and who would manage to fight back and survive for a long period of time.

His key indicator was the ability to focus on the positive, even in the worst of environments. While crowded in a boxcar in blinding heat, Dr. Frankl realized he could pray with the people next to him to take their minds off their agony. Locked in barracks with no windows, he found a small crack in the wall that allowed him to see the sky. He would spend hours looking at the sky remembering how beautiful the world was beyond his prison.

Even in a Nazi concentration camp, some people could maintain some degree of optimism and fight back against depression. This means that it must be possible for us to do the same, given that we have far more positive things to focus on than were available to Dr. Frankl. The essential trick is to figure out what those things are.

The disease of depression hijacks the brain and chemically alters its perceptual system. As a result, we have a tendency to focus on and exaggerate the negative things going on around us. If nothing negative is happening, our depressive brain will help us make up negative things to think about. (How many of you spend hours thinking about the awful things that could happen tomorrow or in the future?)

Our depressive brain chemistry also makes it more difficult for us to maintain a focus on the good things going on around us. This is because the depressive brain chemistry inhibits the production of normal levels of pleasure chemicals. As a result, when something good happens to us, we tend to feel only a slight improvement in our mood which quickly subsides, leaving us feeling depressed and empty.

Notice, however, in the above paragraphs I used the words "the depressive-brain chemistry has a tendency to....". Our depressive brain influences but does not control us. It invites us to react in certain ways, but it does not force us to do so. Our depression, however, does make it harder to start feeling good and to keep those good feelings alive. This means we have to develop skills and techniques to jump start the pleasure chemicals in our brain and to keep those pleasure chemicals flowing once they get started. The gratitude list is a tool that can allow us to do just that. It is a written list of all the things for which we are grateful.

Once there was a man who was seriously depressed while driving to work during rush hour traffic. He did not sleep well and had a very hard time dragging himself out of bed. He ended up leaving for work fifteen minutes late and getting caught in unusually heavy traffic that would make him even later.

He started talking to himself, saying things like, "I knew this would happen. Whenever I try to get better, something always screws it up—if it is not the traffic, it is something else! Nothing ever has or will go right for me and this is just one example. If I keep showing up late, I will get fired and there is nothing I can do about it because my depression is so bad. I can't manage my life."

As he sat there, his depression deepened and he started thinking life was not worth living and that he would be better off dead. But then he did something he had never done before. He had started in therapy for depression several weeks previously and his therapist had described the process of building a gratitude list by focusing on the positive things that were happening in his life. His therapist also told him it would not be easy to get started; he would have to "jump start" his mind to focus on something positive.

The man hated the way he was feeling and decided to give the process a try. Here is what he did:

First, he looked out the window and noticed the sun was shining—it was a beautiful day. Then he said to himself, "I am grateful it is a beautiful day and that the sun is shining." He felt silly doing it, but he was so desperate that he followed his therapist's advice, even though he really did not want to.

Then he noticed the car he was driving—the driver's seat was very comfortable. So he said to himself that he was grateful to have a car with a comfortable seat. Then he thought about all the people in the world who did not have a car and said to himself, "I am grateful to make enough money to afford a car."

He noticed the music playing on his car CD player and said to himself, "I am grateful to have a nice stereo and my favorite CDs at hand. If I choose to, I can enjoy the music, let go of these negative thoughts, and start feeling a little bit better."

Then he went on to think of some other things he was grateful for, such as a loving wife who was staying with him through his addiction and depression, three children who he loved very much and who brought a great deal of joy into his life, and a good paying job that allowed him to support his family in a decent fashion. Finally, he noted he was grateful for the therapist and the members of the Twelve-Step group he was attending who were helping him to minimize his depression by refocusing his thoughts.

By the time he completed this mental exercise of creating a gratitude list in his own mind, he found he started feeling a little bit better and the depressive thoughts that normally ran through his mind were beginning to let go and fall into the background of his thinking. He also noticed he was only two exits from his job and would not be nearly as late as he originally thought.

Later that day, he wrote a formal gratitude list on a sheet of paper and kept it with him to read. He felt this would be helpful if he ever had trouble thinking about the good things in his life that he was grateful for.

Tool #12: Make a List of Pleasurable Activities

Think of all the things you have ever done that have made you feel good and write them down. Include both the big pleasures of life, such as loving and being loved, and the small pleasures of life, such as watching a sunset, swimming in a calm lake or ocean, or watching an enjoyable movie.

After you have written down as many pleasant events as you can remember, evaluate each of them using a ten-point scale with 1 being very little pleasure and 10 being the most pleasure you have ever experienced. Then rate how easy it would be do to the activity on an average day, with a 0 being that you would be unable to do it on most days and a 10 being, if you choose to, you could do it on most days.

The entries on your list will look something like this:

Pleasurable Activity	How good does it make you feel?	How easy would it be to do it on most days?	How strongly motivated are you to schedule doing it on a regular basis?
1. Watching a Sunset	Pleasure = 3	Ease = 8	Motivation = 1

This entry shows that this person identifies watching a sunset as a pleasurable experience. Watching the sunset creates a good feeling (pleasure rating) of 3 out of a possible 10. It would be relatively easy to watch the sunset on most days with an ease rating of

156

8 out of a possible 10. Unfortunately, this person has a very low level of desire to go out and watch sunsets as indicated by his motivation rating of 1 out of a possible 10.

Keep a daily rating of all your activities and rate the pleasure level of everything you do. Review your list each evening before you go to bed and each morning as you plan your day. Ask yourself, "How can I eliminate as many unpleasant activities as possible? How can I schedule as many pleasurable activities as possible? How can I increase the good feelings involved in the activities I need to schedule into my life?"

Tool #13: Recognize the Voice of Your Depression

Before you can learn to effectively manage your depression, you need to learn about the voices of depression and addiction that talk with you in the privacy of your own mind. We all talk, argue, and debate with ourselves. Whenever we develop a serious long-term problem, we also develop an automatic habit of talking to ourselves about the problem. This is normal and natural.

The process of talking with yourself is called *self-talk*. A thought just pops into your mind. Then another thought comes to mind that answers or argues with the first voice. This leads to having a conversation with yourself. These inner conversations are called *inner dialogues*. Each voice in the dialogue represents deeply entrenched habits of thinking that you have developed. These thoughts can become habitual or automatic. A trigger goes off and the thoughts just pop into your head. Once they get started, it can be hard to stop or redirect them. The thoughts often spiral out of control like they have a life of their own. It can become so bad that it feels like the voices have taken over your mind. Research shows that when people learn to identify and change their self-talk, they can decrease the severity of their depression and start to feel better.

When we have serious problems like addiction and depression, we develop automatic thoughts that have only one purpose—to keep us from solving or effectively managing the problem. Fortunately, we also have a healthy voice that helps us recognize these voices and fight back.

As a result, you can learn to use self-talk and inner dialogue to recognize and manage the depressive voices that constantly run through your head. You can learn to change your self-talk and inner dialogue in a way that will help you feel better, stay sober, and responsibly handle your life. The process works like this.

Step 1: Prepare: Get a pencil and paper. Find a quiet place where you can sit down and be alone for a few minutes.

Step 2: Relax and Get Centered: Take a deep breath, hold it for a moment, and then exhale. Begin breathing in a slow and comfortable way. With each breath, allow yourself to become still and quiet.

Step 3: Clear Your Mind: Focus on your breathing and try to clear your mind of all thoughts.

Step 4: Notice Your Thoughts: Notice when you start saying something to yourself. When a thought pops into your head, just notice it. Say to yourself, "That's interesting," and then write it down. Then let the thought go by saying to yourself, "I don't need to think about this right now. I can let this thought go." Then focus on your breathing again until another thought comes into your mind. Continue the process until you have a list of seven to ten thoughts that popped into your mind.

Step 5: Label Your Thoughts: If we're trying to recover from depression and addiction, we have both a ***Depressive Voice*** and an ***Addictive Voice*** that talk to us on a regular basis: The purpose of our depressive voice is to keep us so depressed that we're dysfunctional. The purpose of our addictive voice is to make us want to use alcohol or other drugs. These two voices form a partnership to persuade us that we are so miserable that we need to drink and use drugs in order to feel better.

Fortunately, we all have a third voice in our head which I call the ***Healthy Self*** or the ***Higher Self***. This voice does one of two things: it either makes us feel a little bit better right now or it encourages us to make plans to start feeling better in the future even though we really don't want to right now. In other words, the higher self gives us the courage, strength, and hope to keep doing positive things despite our depression. The higher self gives us the courage to rise above our depression and do what we need to do to get well despite our depression.

As human beings, we are capable of self-programming. Our past does not have to determine our future. We don't have to blindly react to our depression in ways that make it worse. We can ask for help, think it through, make a plan, and then do what we need to do even if our addictive and depressive selves don't want us to.

> **The Higher Self gives us...**
>
> **1. Courage, strength, and hope to keep doing positive things despite our depression.**
>
> **2. Courage to rise above our depression and do what we need to do to get well despite our depression.**

When you notice that thoughts are running through your mind, ask yourself three questions:

1.   Is thinking this thought going to make me more depressed? If the answer is "Yes," it's a depressive thought.

2.   Is thinking this thought going to make me want to use alcohol or other drugs? If the answer is "Yes," it's an addictive thought.

3.   Is thinking this thought making me feel a little bit better right now or is it encouraging me to make a plan to do things that will make me feel better in the near future? If the answer to this question is "Yes," you've made contact with your healthy self that wants you to stay sober, feel better, and have meaning and purpose in life.

Step 6: Get to Know Your Depressive Self: Depressive thinking can become an automatic and unconscious habit that slowly becomes a part of your personality. Depressive thinking has two purposes: to make you feel depressed and to keep you feeling depressed. The depressive voice in your head will justify your depression and keep you depressed no matter what you do.

> **Depressive thinking has two purposes:**
> 1. **To make you feel depressed**
> 2. **To keep you feeling depressed**

Here are some of the most common depressive thoughts:

- I'm worthless and defective!
- My life is awful, terrible, and unbearable!
- I'm helpless!
- It's hopeless!
- There is nothing I can do to change myself or my life!
- Nothing will ever get better—I'll be this way forever!
- Things will just keep getting worse!
- Nobody can help me!
- If others could help, they'd choose not to!
- This will never end!
- There's no way out!
- I can't stand it!
- I'd be better off dead!

Our depressive illness makes us more likely to think depressive thoughts. Our depressive thoughts make our depressive illness worse. It's a vicious circle. Fortunately, we also have a part of ourselves that is hopeful, joyful, and serene.

Step 7: Get to Know Your Addictive Self: Addictive thinking can also become an automatic and unconscious habit that interacts with your depressive thinking. Addictive thinking has three purposes:

to make you so miserable in sobriety that you want to drink and use drugs, to provide excuses and justifications for starting to use alcohol and other drugs, and to keep you using once you start. In other words, the only purpose of your addictive self is to keep itself alive while destroying you.

The addictive voice in your head will justify using alcohol and other drugs no matter what the consequences. The primary tool of the addictive self is what I call *The Big Lie of Addiction:* alcohol and other drugs are my friends who will make my depression go away and help me to have a better life. Alcohol and drugs don't make depression any better; they make it worse. We might feel better for a few minutes, but most of us don't. I've talked with many people who have relapsed to alcohol and drugs in an attempt to feel less depressed. Most were very disappointed. They barely got any relief before they lost control of their addiction, and the addiction and depression, working together as a team, drove them into a pit of depression and started tearing apart what was left of their lives.

The Big Lie of Addiction: **alcohol and other drugs are my friends who will make my depression go away and help me to have a better life.**

Step 8: Discover Your Higher Self: The higher self gives you a set of automatic thoughts that makes you feel excited rather than depressed, hopeful rather than hopeless, joyful rather than sad, and serene instead of agitated. You can find optimistic thoughts to offset every depressive thought. The higher self helps you rise above your depression and do things that will make you feel a little bit better right now. The higher self then gives you the energy to develop a recovery plan that slowly helps you manage and overcome your depression one day at a time while maintaining your sobriety.

The following table contains a list of the common depressive things you can say to yourself to challenge those thoughts and shut down the depressive self. Make a copy of it. Hang it on your bathroom mirror. Carry it with you and read it at least four times a day (morning, noon, dinnertime, and before you go to bed). Force yourself to read the list whether you feel like it or not. If possible, read the list out loud with energy and conviction in your voice. In other words, put some feeling and energy behind it. Imagine that you have been captured by a terrorist who has a gun to your head and tells you to read the list convincingly into a camera or you will be shot.

Depressive Thoughts	Optimistic Thoughts
1. I'm worthless!	1. *I am not worthless.* I am feeling so bad that it's hard for me to appreciate my value, but it's there. **Assignment:** Write a list of all the things you do that are helpful and contribute something of value to others.
2. I'm defective and can't do anything right!	2. *I am not defective.* I may be suffering from depression, but I am still able to do many things that contribute to those around me. I may have limitations, but so does everyone even if they're not depressed. **Assignment:** Write a list of all the things you are able to do well.
3. My life is awful, terrible, and unbearable!	3. *My life is not awful, terrible, and unbearable.* I have problems that are inconvenient and frustrating, but I'll be able to figure out how to handle them. **Assignment:** Identify five items in your life that frustrate you. Evaluate each problem on a ten-point scale with 10 being a problem that can destroy you and your life and 1 being a minor inconvenience.

4. I'm helpless!	4. *I am not helpless.* There are things I'm not able to do, but I can get people to help me. There are many things I'm able to do despite my depression. **Assignment:** Write down all the excuses you use for not trying to do things. Write a list of ten things that you are capable of doing despite your depression.
5. It's hopeless!	5. *It is not hopeless.* Hope comes from being able to see the possibility of a positive outcome. My depression makes it difficult for me to believe things will come out well, but some things do. **Assignment:** Write down three things that have worked out well in the past several weeks.
6. There is nothing that I can do to change myself or my life!	6. *There are some things I can do to change myself.* There are many little things that I can do to make myself feel a little bit better. **Assignment:** Write down three things you can do to feel a little bit better. List simple things like taking a bath, going for a walk, watching your favorite TV show, reading a book, etc.

7. Nothing will ever get better—I'll be this way forever!	7. *Things will get better; this will not last forever.* Life tends to progress in cycles. Problems come up, things seem impossible, then you do something or something happens in your life that makes things better. **Assignment:** Think of some things in your past, perhaps when you were a child or adolescent, that you believed would never get better and then they did. Make a list of all the problems that you think will never get better. Read each problem out loud and then say to yourself, "This, too, shall pass."
8. Things will just keep getting worse!	8. *Things might get worse, but I'll be able to handle whatever happens.* I can do things that will increase the likelihood that things will get better. **Assignment:** Write a list of all the things you can do to make things worse. Next to each item write something you could do to make it a little better.
9. Nobody can help me!	9. *Some people will refuse to help me, but others will be willing to help.* It is my

	job to seek out the help I need and not be discouraged if the first people I ask can't or won't help me.
	Assignment: Write down all the excuses you use for not trying to do things. Write a list of ten things that you are capable of doing despite your depression.
10. If others could help, they'd choose not to!	10. *Some people may refuse to help me, but there are people who will help me if I'm willing to ask.* There is always someplace to go to get help. All I have to do is keep looking until I find it.
	Assignment: Go to a telephone book and make a list of all of the community mental health centers and therapists who work with people suffering from depression.
11. This will never end!	11. *All things, both good and bad, come to an end.* Life is a cycle of beginnings and endings.
	Assignment: Whenever you catch yourself saying, "This will never end," force yourself to say, "This, too, shall pass."

12. There's no way out!	12. *There's always a way out.* Sometimes you need to find a comfortable and relaxed place within yourself. Things always change and if you can stay calm and centered, you can notice the opportunities that those changes bring. **Assignment:** Make a list of the problems that are trapping you. Next to each problem write a description of a possible way out of that problem. Interview three other people who have been trapped by similar problems but managed to deal with them effectively. Find out what they did.
13. I can't stand it!	13. *I can stand it.* Things may cause me to feel uncomfortable, frustrated, or hurt. This is inconvenient, but I can handle it. **Assignment:** List at least one difficult experience in your life that you thought you couldn't stand yet dealt with effectively.
14. I'd be better off dead!	14. **This definitely isn't true.** Dying is never a solution. Depression can make you feel so bad that

	you want to die, but there are many ways to feel better without killing yourself. **Assignment:** Always take thoughts of suicide seriously, tell your family, and make an appointment with a therapist. Remember that you are needed and wanted. List all the people in your life who would be seriously hurt if you killed yourself. List three specific things that are making you want to die. Talk to a friend or therapist about what you can do to manage those things.

As you can see, it is possible to learn how to identify and challenge depressive thoughts and beliefs. You can learn to replace those false beliefs with accurate beliefs. When these mistaken beliefs pop into your head, you can challenge them by telling yourself the truth. Here are some of the things you can say to yourself to challenge the mistaken beliefs.

Challenge #1: *I'm not powerless.*

Many of us believe we're powerless. This is not true. No matter how bad we feel, there is always something we can do to make ourselves feel a little bit better. We can also do things that will make us feel a little bit worse. The choice is ours, but it's not hopeless.

Challenge #2: Other people have beat depression and I can, too.

Many of us mistakenly believe that nobody can recover from depression. This simply is not true. Many people learn to effectively manage their depression. They make the choices to do things that start making themselves feel a little bit better. They don't get demoralized by temporary setbacks. They learn from their mistakes. Slowly the depression begins to lift, and as an added benefit, they have meaningful and satisfying lives.

Challenge #3: There are things I can do that will help me to start feeling better.

Many of us believe there is nothing we can do to effectively manage our depression. If we're depressed, we just need to sit back and stay depressed until we start feeling better. This is not true. There are things we can do that will slowly relieve our depression over time. We need to consistently do these things, and this requires a recovery program. A recovery program is a schedule of things that we do every day to combat our depression. We can build a recovery program that will work for us and then put time and energy into our recovery program whether we feel like it or not.

Challenge #4: There are people who love and care about me and are willing and able to help.

The biggest mistaken belief that can take us into the depths of depression is the cluster of related mistaken beliefs that go like this: "Nobody cares about me. Nobody is capable of helping me. Even if they were able to help, they wouldn't do it." This cluster of beliefs is not true.

We all have people who love and care about us. We can all find other people, both professionals and those in support groups like the Twelve-Step programs, who will support us as we move ahead in our recovery. We don't need to let our depression ruin those relationships. We can stay connected and keep reaching out even though we feel depressed.

Challenge #5: There are things that are worth living for.

The final mistaken belief is that life isn't worth living. When we are trapped by this mistaken belief, we focus on our depression and block out everything else. We all have a mission and a purpose in life that is ours and ours alone. We don't need to let our depression rob us of that meaning and purpose. We all have the capacity for joy and transcendence. We are all able to find moments during which we can rise above our depression and the circumstances of life to find a sense of meaning and purpose.

If nothing else, we have many things to teach others. Our life experiences have value, and the process of sharing them, especially with people who are younger than us, can help us to reassess our life experiences and assign new meaning to them. This can help us feel better about ourselves and our lives. Remember the promise of Alcoholics Anonymous (AA): *No matter how far down the scale we have gone, we will find that our experiences can be valuable to others.*

Tool #14: Learning to Monitor Your Depressive Thoughts

Most depressed people are really good at getting depressed. They know exactly what to think and do to make themselves feel awful. One of the exercises I use in my training workshops is this: I ask people to rate their current level of depression on a scale from 0 to 10 and write it down on a sheet of paper.

Then I ask them to take exactly one minute to raise their level of depression as high as they can. Most people find that they can increase their depression by three to five points in a minute. Then I ask them to write down what they did to increase their feelings. What thoughts did you think? What memories did you call to mind? What future situations did you begin to think about? How did you change your facial expressions and body posture?

Then I break the participants into small groups to share their results and create a list of things that you could do if you wanted to get really depressed. Most groups come up with a long, comprehensive list of instructions for getting really depressed. Once they discover what they do to make themselves depressed, they have the power to choose to stop doing those things and to do something else.

I ask people to take another minute to start feeling really good. Surprisingly, most people can't change their depression by more than one or two points in the positive direction. Many even get more depressed as they do things to try and feel better. Depressed people, it seems, don't have very many effective skills for feeling good.

I have them write a list describing all the things they did to try and make themselves feel better and get into their groups and combine the lists. The list of ways to feel better is usually much shorter than the list of ways to get more depressed. This means that if you're depressed, you have to take special effort to learn, practice, and consistently use ways of thinking, feeling, acting, and relating to others in a way that makes you feel better while tuning down or turning off the symptoms of your depression.

Monitoring Depressive Thoughts

It's important to remember that depression is driven by five automatic depressive thoughts. You've learned these thoughts so well that they come into your mind automatically and turn on the depression switch in your brain and then disappear so quickly that you don't even notice they were there. These five thoughts are as follows:

Depressive Thoughts

1. **I'm helpless!** (I'm so depressed I can't do anything.)

2. **It's hopeless!** (My depression is so bad there is absolutely nothing I can do to make my life even a little bit better.)

3. **It will always be this way!** (No matter what I do nothing will ever change.)

4. **No one can help me!** (Nobody really knows anything that can help me manage my depression more effectively. Even if others could help me, they probably wouldn't.)

5. **I'm worthless!** (I'm a worthless person who deserves to feel exactly how I feel [depressed] and have the kind of life I have [a life dominated by hopelessness and devoid of meaning, purpose, and hope].)

These are the thoughts that ultimately lead us into the trap of depression and keep us there. The good news is that we can learn to notice these thoughts as they invade our minds and switch on the faulty brain circuit called depression. Learning to notice these depressive thoughts isn't that hard to do. Try these three simple but not easy steps:

Step 1: Make a Deck of Depressive Thought Cards: Make a photocopy of the box that lists the depressive thoughts and cut it out. You can also write these thoughts neatly on a three-by-five-inch card. Some people laminate the cards to protect them, just like we use denial and blame to protect the real depressive thoughts we carry in our heads.

Step 2: Carry the cards with you: Carry the cards with you just like you carry these depressive thoughts with you in your mind all of the time. Keep them readily available in a pocket, your wallet, or a purse. Put them in a place where they keep getting in the way, just like the real depressive thoughts keep getting in your way.

Step 3: Use the cards to notice your depressive thoughts: This is called self-monitoring. Pull out the cards and read these thoughts every time you think about it. You should think about them a lot, because you're keeping the cards in a place where they keep getting in the way. Every time you read the cards, notice how these thoughts make you feel. Do they make you feel more or less depressed? Is this the way you want to feel?

Use a daily mood diary to record your habitual ways of thinking that lead to depressive thoughts. List how you feel when you get up in the morning, before and after each major scheduled event, and before you go to bed at night. Use a scale that goes from a minus ten (-10) indicating the worst that you could ever feel, to a plus ten (+10) indicating the best you could possibly feel. This exercise will help you stay aware of the changes in your mood and how your daily activities affect your mood. This information can help you make better choices about what types of things you should do during each day to feel as good as possible.

A Daily Mood Diary would look like this:

Time	Activity	Pleasure Rating: (-10–+10)
6:00 a.m.	Alarm went off. Decided to go back to sleep instead of getting up to exercise.	Before: -8
		After: -8
8:00 a.m.	Forced self to get out of bed and get to work. No time to shower or eat breakfast. Agitated and depressed during drive. Afraid I would be late.	Before: -8
		After: -9
9:15 a.m.–Noon	Arrived 15 minutes late for work. No one noticed. Worked hard but felt bored with job and afraid boss would talk to me about being late. Skipped break to make up for being late.	Before: -9
		After: +2

Noon–1:00 p.m.	Lunch. Ate a greasy cheeseburger and fries with a milk-shake. Ended up with an upset stomach.	Before: +2
		After: -3
1:00–5:00 p.m.	Worked all afternoon at boring tasks. I hate this job, but I'm trapped.	Before: -3
		After: -6
5:00–8:00 p.m.	Went home. Ate junk food because I was too depressed to make dinner. Hate being alone.	Before: -6
		After: -8
8:00 p.m.–1:00 a.m.	Decided to stay home and watch TV instead of going to an AA meeting. Why bother? Nothing is going to change. Channel surfed. Nothing interested me.	Before: -8
		After: -9
1:00–6:00 a.m.	Slept fitfully. Awoke many times. Alarm went off at 6:00 a.m. I still feel tired. Here we go again. It's showtime.	Before: -9
		After: -9

Tool #15: Set a Vision for Recovery

Perhaps the most important question that needs to be thought through in managing depression is this: *What do you want your life to be like when you have successfully learned to manage your depression?*

This is an important question for a number of reasons. First, by asking it of yourself, thinking about, going into states of quiet reflection, and waiting for

176

answers to emerge within your mind, you automatically begin assuming an attitude of hope. You will be suggesting to yourself that you will learn how to manage your depression and this will put your creative mind to work on finding solutions.

The second thing this question does is shift your mind away from placing depression as the central issue in your life. When I ask most depressed people what they want their life to be like when they have learned to manage their depression, most say they want the depression to be gone. In a way this makes sense, but think about it deeply for a moment: "When my depression is gone, I want my depression to be gone." That's OK, but what else do you want from your life? Depression lives in the dark, negative void of hopelessness. Without a positive, compelling vision of what you want from life that would give you a sense of meaning and purpose, you are keeping yourself in the psychological trap that feeds your depression.

Think about it and make a list of what you would want from life if you weren't so depressed. Here's my list:

What do I want to have when my depression is no longer the central issue that controls my life?

1. I want a loving relationship with my wife.
2. I want an active and involved relationship with my children.
3. I want an exciting career that I can pursue while maintaining my health and vitality.
4. I want involvement with interesting and exciting people.
5. I want the challenge of making my community a better place to live.

6. I want the joy and struggle of mentoring younger people in my profession so I can pass on my knowledge and wisdom.
7. I want to keep writing dynamic and creative books that help people learn vital skills in managing their lives more effectively.
8. I want to keep learning new and more effective skills for managing my depression and other personal problems.
9. I want to live consciously and creatively so that my experiences can be of help to others.
10. I want to leave a legacy that demonstrates that one person can make a difference and that every person should try.

Notice, the only thing I want that directly mentions depression is number 8, and that involves continuous work at learning new and more effective ways to keep my depression from getting in the way of other, more important things in my life.

Treating depression is about a lot more than just not being depressed. Treating depression is about finding a way to put meaning and purpose into your life despite your depression.

Treating depression is about a lot more than just not being depressed. Treating depression is about finding a way to put meaning and purpose into your life despite your depression.

Once you write out your list that captures your personal vision of recovery, look at it carefully and ask yourself these questions:

1. Am I doing any of these things now despite my depression?

If I am, why am I focusing my mind on the actions of a faulty brain circuit that robs me of energy and makes me feel helpless, hopeless, and disconnected from others?

2. If I am not doing any of these things, why not? What's stopping me?

The answer to this question will probably boil down to one of several different reasons or excuses.

Excuse #1: I'm not doing these things because my mind is so fogged by my depression that I can't bring anything positive into mind. Depression 1, Recovering person 0.

Excuse #2: Even if I can think of some positive things to do, my depression is so bad that I won't be able to do it? Depression 2, Recovering person 0.

Excuse #3: Even if I could do these things, they probably wouldn't work for me. Nothing ever works for me. Notice the underlying hopelessness in this answer reflecting the unexpressed thought *nothing will ever change*. Also notice the use of emotional reasoning: If it doesn't feel good now, it isn't worth doing. The only thing of value is what feels good in the moment. There is nothing more enduring or sustaining in life than what I feel right now. So if I don't feel good about doing something, or don't feel like doing something, it isn't worth doing. *Depression 3, Recovering person 0. Three strikes and you're out.* You've allowed your depression to win control of your life and you haven't even made the attempt to fight back. Is that really the way you want the rest of your life to go?

The key question is this: *Why don't we do the things we need to do in order to feel better?* There is only one valid answer to this question: "I refuse to try! I'm giving my depression so much power that I'm letting it control my mind, my spirit, and my life. I have come to mistakenly believe that my depression is so powerful there is absolutely nothing I can do to fight back. And so instead of trying to figure out things I could do to feel better, I turn control of my life over to my depression. I give up other values that are strong enough to overcome my depression. I let my depression destroy my marriage, relationship with my children, friendships, positive community involvement, helping others, making a contribution, and leaving a legacy.

I turn over my power to my depression in three ways:

1.   By using emotional reasoning. (If it doesn't feel good in the moment it isn't good and therefore it's not worth doing.)

2.   By refusing to set or even think about setting positive goals that could provide a sense of meaning and purpose in my life despite feeling depressed. (My depression is so bad I couldn't do anything of value even if I wanted to, so I'll just stop wanting to.)

3.   By believing that nothing will ever change, no matter what I do, I will always feel depressed and that unless my depression totally goes away there is nothing of value that I could ever accomplish.

Tool #16: Identify the Secondary Gains of Depression

Secondary gains are the positive things that depression is doing for us. As human beings, we are goal-seeking creatures. This means that we tend to use all our experiences, both positive and negative, as tools in meeting our goals and getting what we want.

Depression can become a very powerful tool for convincing others to give us what we want and need. The more serious the depression, the more powerful it is as a tool of social manipulation. Whether we like to admit it or not, we all receive some benefits from our depression.

Many times our depression is aggravated because we have made commitments to people that force us to put ourselves and our needs on the back burner. We work so hard, spend so much time meeting the needs of others, and spend so little time taking care of ourselves that our depression is either activated or made worse by the stress.

The depression can also give us an excuse to stop doing many of the things we don't want to do but don't have the courage to openly refuse to do. The depression can also be a way of getting other people to give us more time and attention without having to directly ask for it and risk rejection.

We can use the depression as an excuse to avoid going to work, to stop working around the house, to get our partners to take on more than their fair share of the boring but necessary tasks of making a household work.

We can use our depression as an excuse for almost any unacceptable or irresponsible behavior. When someone confronts or challenges us we simply say, "You've got to understand, I'm too depressed to do things like that!" In early recovery from depression we do need others to help us out so we can put time and energy into our recovery. If, however, we get other people to do things for us and do nothing to recover from our depression, these people will get angry with us, and they have every right to.

The secondary gains of depression can create an obstacle to recovery. If you're not willing to recognize the needs that are being met by your depression, you can't make a decision to get those needs met in another way. As a result, your depression will get worse.

Here are some questions that can help you determine the secondary gains you are getting from being depressed.

1.   When you get depressed, what routine tasks in life do you tend to stop doing? Make the list as complete as possible and then arrange the items in order from those you tend to give up first when you start feeling depressed to those things you refuse to give up unless your depression is so severe you can't function.

2.   When you get depressed, what relationships in your life are most affected? Make a list of everyone who is affected in either a positive or negative way. It's best to take a sheet of paper, draw a line down the middle, and list the people affected in a positive way by your depression in column 1 (this is usually a very short list) and those affected in a negative way in column 2.

3.   Make a list of all the people you're angry with. Compare these people to the people on your list who are negatively affected by your depression. Sometimes we can use our depression as a weapon to get back at people we are angry with while avoiding the responsibility for what we're doing.

4.   What social and recreational activities do you tend to give up when you get depressed? Depression

can be an effective tool for getting us out of things we don't want to do without taking responsibility for it.

5.   What goals would you set for yourself if you weren't so depressed? It's easy to use depression as an excuse for giving up dreams and refusing to try and meet your needs and wants. It's easy to say, "I'm too depressed to take the chance on going after what I really want in life!" The true statement often goes like this: "I'm using my depression to avoid the risk of trying and then failing."

6.   In what ways would your life be different if you weren't suffering from depression and were able to live a normal life?

7.   Why can't you start making positive changes in your life even though you're depressed? As one of my friends once told me, "It's just as easy to be depressed sitting at a Twelve-Step meeting as it is sitting in front of my television set surfing the channels. The only difference is I'm much more likely to feel better after sitting through a meeting than after watching television."

It's just as easy to be depressed sitting at a Twelve-Step meeting as it is sitting in front of my television set surfing the channels.

The only difference is I'm much more likely to feel better after sitting through a meeting than after watching TV.

If you think there are some secondary gains you're getting from being depressed, make a list. Then set up a plan to get each secondary gain without being depressed. You may not be able to do it all at once, but at least you will be able to separate, in your own mind, the difference between the consequences of your depression and the consequences of using your depression as an excuse for not meeting the challenges of your life.

There is a difference between the negative consequences of your depression and the negative consequences of using your depression as an excuse for not meeting the challenges of your life.

If you don't identify the secondary gains you get from your depression, you might relapse back into depression just as your recovery program is starting to work. Why? Because we mistakenly believe if we give up our depression, we must also give up our ability to get other things we want in life.

Tool #17: Stop Using Your Depression as an Excuse

There is no such thing as being too depressed to do things that will help you to feel a little bit better right now. We're constantly trying to do things to help us cope with our depression. The problem is that we often do the wrong things for the right reasons. At other times we just choose not to try. The truth is this: we choose to turn our lives over to our depression by refusing to take responsibility for learning new skills and taking action. Every time we decide to let our depression win the battle, it gets stronger by feeding off of our life energy. As a result, our depression gets worse. Every time we decide to do something to make ourselves feel a little bit less depressed, our depression loses the battle and gets a little bit weaker. As a result, there is more life energy left for us to use to take the next step in getting even a little bit better.

> **Depression is effectively managed by making small decisions that make us feel a little better right now, and then repeating that process many times each day.**

Depression is effectively managed by making small decisions that make us feel a little better right now, and then repeating that process many times each day.

Depression is not managed by making a single dramatic decision. Depression is effectively managed by making small decisions to make you feel a little better many times each day. Each of these little decisions is important, because over time they add up to major changes in your ability to manage depression and live normally.

Tool #18: Challenge Your Depressive Thinking

If you don't like how these thoughts make you feel, learn how to challenge them. In the following boxes I've written an example of how you can challenge each depressive thought. You can copy and cut these cards out and carry them with you. As you read each depressive thought, emotionally disempower it by realizing that it's not true, then read the thought that directly challenges it. Empower the challenging thoughts by forcing yourself to put some strong emotion behind the thought when you read it. Many people find it helpful to write a personal version of each challenging thought that is easier for them to remember and to get psyched up about. In the boxes below I've written some ideas about how you can challenge each thought. (Remember, your depression will make you want to stop reading and give up. Who will you allow to win—your depressive self or your recovering self?)

If you choose to learn how to challenge your depressive thoughts, it's important to read the list of depressive thoughts and the challenges for each thought at least four times per day (in the morning when you get up, during your lunch break, during your dinner time, and before bed). After you read the depressive thoughts and healthy challenges, get quiet, centered, and think back since your last reading of the card. Did you notice any of these depressive thoughts invading your mind? (You must notice them before you can challenge them.) Did you just give in to these thoughts when you noticed them or did you try to challenge them? If you tried to challenge them, how well did it work? Remember that your goal is progress not perfection. Your goal is to learn how to make yourself feel a little bit better instead of a little bit worse. Your depressive voice will try to tell you that since this process didn't instantly and totally take away all of your depression, it's a waste of time. After all, you're helpless and there's no point in trying. Do you see the trap? Remember, depression is a cunning opponent.

·

Challenging Depressive Thoughts

1. **I'm Helpless!** (I'm so depressed I can't do anything.)

- **No, I am not helpless.** I may feel depressed but there are things I can do to make myself feel a little bit better if I choose to do them. (Then think of some of the things you could do.)

2. **It's Hopeless!** (My depression is so bad there is absolutely nothing I can do to make my life even a little bit better.)

- **No, it's not hopeless.** I can choose to believe it's hopeless and use this as an excuse for making myself feel worthless. Or I can choose to get off the pity pot and start forcing myself to do some little things that could make me feel a little bit better.

3. **It will always be this way!** (No matter what I do nothing will ever change.)

- **No, it won't always be this way.** My life is in a constant state of change. I am just choosing to let these thoughts activate a defective depressive brain circuit and then I allow the defective circuit to run my life. I can stop doing this every so often. I can make small changes every day that will start to make my life better.

4. **No one can help me!** (Nobody really knows anything that can help me manage my depression more effectively. Even if others could help me, they probably wouldn't.)

- **This isn't true. There are people who are willing and able to help me.** Depression is one of the most common mental disorders in the country and people learn to effectively manage it all the time. There are skilled therapists in every community who can help me learn science-based skills for managing depression if I reach out and ask for help. There are also programs in nearly every church in the country that teach the spiritual skills of moving from hopelessness to hopefulness through faith in God or a Higher Power. Help is available if I'm willing to look for it and invest my time, energy, and resources to get it.

5. **I'm Worthless!** (I'm a worthless person who deserves to feel exactly how I feel [depressed] and who deserves to have the kind of life I have [a life dominated by hopelessness and devoid of meaning, purpose, and hope].)

- **No, I'm not worthless!** How I feel does not determine my worth as a human being. Some of the people who made the biggest contributions to humanity suffered from depression, but they kept in touch with their sense of value and their ability to make a contribution despite their depression.

The more you practice identifying and challenging your depressive thoughts, the easier it will get. I suggest that you have practice sessions at least four times a day with each session lasting between five and fifteen minutes. At each practice session, you should take out your recovery journal and turn to the section where you have been keeping track of your depressive thoughts and how to challenge them. Select different thoughts and start running them through your mind. Then consciously challenge them. Argue back and forth with them until they completely go away.

If you do this, you will probably become more aware of all the depressive thoughts that pop into your mind that you never noticed before. As you notice these thoughts, challenge them just like you would in a practice session. As this occurs, your focus will shift from practicing the thoughts in an artificial session to actually doing battle with the depressive thoughts as they try to invade your mind. This exercise will give you skills at managing depressive thoughts. It will also help you develop the habit of awareness. You'll be surprised when you start to notice how often these depressive thoughts silently invade your mind and start activating or intensifying your depression.

Whenever you notice the thought, ask yourself this question: *Do I want to turn my mind, spirit, and life over to a faulty brain circuit that makes me think depressive thoughts?* If you don't, you now have the ability to consciously fight back. It's always your choice, and the battle is never easy, but if you work at it consistently, the process works and starts to become easier.

Tool #19: Recognize that Depression Can Be Your Friend

Realize that your depression is giving you a wake-up call. *Here is your wake-up call: Y*ou may feel depressed, but you are not helpless, hopeless, and powerless. You are not useless and incompetent. You don't have to empower your depression and disempower the real you.

Physical pain isn't bad. Pain makes us uncomfortable, but it has a vital purpose. Physical pain can be a friend that tells us when we're physically injured or sick and motivates us to do what's necessary to recover. Depression is just like physical pain. Depression can be a friend that tells us when we're in trouble psychologically. Most people get depressed because they have a lot of things to be depressed about. You can turn your problems with depression into a wake-up call that motivates you to evaluate and change your life for the better. If you're depressed, it's usually because of a combination of physical, psychological, and social problems that prevent you from finding meaning, purpose, and satisfaction in your life. Your depression can become a friend that pushes you out of the old habits that are slowly killing you. Your depression can force you to evaluate and change how you are living your life.

Part 9:
The Twelve
Steps of
Depression

It's important to remember that the Twelve Steps are a program that produces good, solid mental health. There are two Twelve-Step programs that have demonstrated success with depression: Neurotics Anonymous (Mail Stop 102, San Francisco, CA 94111) and Emotions Anonymous (on the Internet at *http://www.emotionsanonymous.org*). Both of these programs are successful self-help groups with a long history of providing help and support for people recovering from depression. These programs apply the Twelve Steps to problems of emotional management including depression. For our purposes, however, we can easily rewrite the Twelve Steps to focus on depression. Here's what these steps look like:

Step 1: I Can't

Step 1

We admitted we're powerless over depression, that our lives have become unmanageable.

In the First Step, we admit that we can't control our depression and that our depression is causing serious life problems. These problems are hurting people we love and care about. We also admit that we have tried everything we know how to do in order to manage our depression, but nothing has worked. We've lost control of our depression, we're suffering, and our life is being disrupted.

Loss of control doesn't mean that our depression causes life problems all of the time. It means that we periodically have episodes of depression that prevent us from functioning normally. It also means that we can never be sure when an episode of severe depression will be activated, rear its ugly head, and disrupt our ability to function.

To work the First Step in relation to your depression, take a sheet of paper and fold it in half, making two long columns. At the top of the first column write: *Symptoms of depression I have experienced.* At the top of column two write, *How this symptom caused problems in my life.* To fill out column #1, go back to the Depression Symptom Checklist (see page 58–59) and use that to do a personal inventory. Next to each symptom, write about what happens when you experience that symptom. What do you do that hurts others? What are you unable to do that causes you to be irresponsible?

Until you fully recognize that you have depression and that it is a serious problem disrupting your life, you probably won't be able to motivate yourself to take action.

Step 2: Somebody Else Can

> ### Step 2
>
> *Came to believe*
> *that a Power greater than ourselves*
> *could restore us to sanity.*

In Step 2 we become open to the possibility that there is someone or something out there that can help us to stay sober, deal with our depression, and effectively manage our lives and our relationships.

At the core of the Second Step is the belief in some kind of Higher Power that is capable of helping us. This is especially difficult for depressed people because they have developed deeply engrained beliefs that life is hopeless, they are helpless, no one cares or has the power to help, and things will never get better.

This is difficult for most of us to do, especially if we're suffering from both addiction and depression. Depression is a disease of helplessness, hopelessness, futility, and isolation. We feel *helpless* because we mistakenly believe that *there's nothing we can do to feel better.* We feel *hopeless* because we mistakenly believe that *nothing can or will ever be different.* We feel *futility* because we mistakenly believe that *no matter what we do, it won't help.* We feel *isolated* because we mistakenly believe that *there is no one and nothing that can ever help us.*

The Second Step asks us to directly challenge these beliefs. Notice that the Step does not say "firmly believed." It says "came to believe." All we need to do to work this Step and open the doorway to hope is to believe that there might be someone out there who is willing and able to help. We need to begin experimenting with a new way of thinking: "Maybe I'm not as helpless as I think I am. Maybe there is a chance I can learn to manage my depression, stay clean and sober, and live a meaningful and comfortable life. Maybe there is someone or something out there willing and able to help."

This new way of thinking will make us willing to look for new solutions and become willing to try new things.

Step 3: I'll Let Them Help Me

> ### Step 3
>
> *Made a decision to turn our will and our lives over to the care of a Higher Power as we understood Him.*

Step 3 tells us to trust in a Higher Power. In Step 2 we came to believe in some source of courage, strength, hope, knowledge, or support that could show us a way to cope with our depression. In Step 3 we need to identify a Higher Power. Then we must become willing to take direction from our new-found Higher Power and see what happens.

But who or what is the Higher Power? The Twelve Steps tell us very clearly that it's up to each of us to find our own Higher Power. In the Twelve-

Step program, the terms Higher Power and God are often used interchangeably. The Twelve-Step program doesn't prescribe a specific concept of God, but rather instructs its members to find a God of their own understanding.

In my understanding, there are three possible things that we can select as a Higher Power. The first is a person who knows more about dealing with addiction and depression than we do. The second is a group of such individuals. The third is the source of knowledge that infuses the individual members and animates the group conscience.

In my understanding, the Higher Power serves two functions. The first is emotional: it gives us the courage, strength, and hope to move ahead in our recovery, not without being depressed but in spite of the fact that we feel depressed. The second function that the Higher Power serves is intellectual and behavioral. It gives us the knowledge of what we need to do. Then it motivates us to do it.

If we have chosen our Higher Power correctly, when we connect with it we will become motivated to learn about what we can do to recover and hope we will be able to find something that works. As addicts, we want a quick fix. We expect instant gratification. Recovery from depression is possible, but it doesn't happen quickly. We slowly recover over days, weeks, and months. Usually our depression doesn't suddenly go away; it ebbs and flows and cycles. Over time the bad times get a little bit better and don't last quite so long. The good times, the times when we are depression free and able to live normally and enjoy life, get better and start lasting longer. It's a slow process of change that requires hope, a plan, flexibility, and patience. Hope allows us to believe we can do something to get better. Developing a plan based on expert advice gives us concrete action steps we can take whether we feel like it or not. Being flexible, we can change or adapt the plan as circumstances change or we become aware of new knowledge and information. Patience gives us the ability to do what we need to do, one day at a time, whether we feel like it or not, even when we feel depressed.

In Step 3 you can select God as your Higher Power, but many people, especially newcomers, don't. They use their Twelve-Step group as their initial Higher Power. The group meets all the criteria. By going to meetings and talking honestly with group members, you can tap into a strong belief that recovery is possible. The power of the group conscience can give you the courage, strength, and hope to go on. By listening to the stories of other group members and participating in Step Study and Big Book meetings, we can learn what we need to do in order to get well. As we work at our recovery we can share our progress and problems with other people who will listen to us, understand our struggles, and take seriously what we are saying.

In Step 1 we said: "I can't do this alone." In Step 2 we opened ourselves up to the possibility that someone else was willing and able to help us. Now, in Step 3, we make a decision to let them help us. We make a decision to follow expert advice whether we want to or not.

Step 4: Taking Inventory

> ### Step 4
>
> *Made a searching and fearless
> moral inventory of ourselves.*

After working the first three Steps, we are into the program. We're willing to listen, accept, and follow suggestions. The first suggestion we receive is contained in Step 4. It suggests we examine ourselves critically to find out who we really are and what we're really doing and not doing in our lives.

The Fourth Step can be a field of land mines for someone with depression. Most Twelve-Step literature tells us to focus on digging up our character defects and short comings. Although we are advised not to focus entirely on the negative, we are given inventory formats that focus on such depressing things as the Seven Deadly Sins of pride, greed, lust, anger, gluttony, envy, and sloth. When we are in the pits of depression, this type of an inventory can amplify our negativity, reinforce the mistaken belief that we're hopeless and helpless, and actually drive us deeper into depression. So what can we do instead?

I suggest an inventory based on the concept of *humility*. Humble people don't build themselves up by trying to appear better than they really are. Nor do humble people tear themselves down by trying to appear worse than they really are. Humble people know who they really are in both their strengths and weaknesses. They are able to act on their strengths and reach out to others to receive help in overcoming their weaknesses.

197

Most depressed people are *grandiose in reverse.* They seek to make themselves seem worse than they really are by doing two things. First, they focus on all of their defects and failings and exaggerate them. Then they block out or minimize all of their strengths and virtues. Then they look at this negatively distorted representation of themselves, believe it's true, and start feeling even more depressed than ever.

So what can we do instead? I suggest doing a Fourth Step Inventory by taking a sheet of paper and folding it in half to create two columns. Across the top of the page write the words *Fourth Step Inventory for Depression.* Underneath that write the definition of humility. The goal of doing a Fourth Step, after all, is to develop a healthy sense of humility. So underneath the words Fourth Step Inventory for Depression write the following: *People with true humility know who they really are in both their strengths and weaknesses. True humility weakens the power of depression.* At the top of column one write the words: *Personal Strengths.* At the top of the second column write the words: *Personal Weaknesses.* The form that we have created will look like this:

Fourth Step Inventory for Depression	
People with true humility know who they really are in both their strengths and weaknesses. True humility weakens the power of depression.	
Personal Strengths	**Personal Weaknesses**

Those of us suffering from depression go right to column two and begin writing a long, exhaustive list of all of our personal weaknesses, both real and imaged. Then we go to column 1 and get stuck. We have a hard time thinking of any personal strengths. The ones that come to mind are often things like the following: *I haven't killed myself yet; I haven't been fired yet;* and so forth.

The first important job in a Fourth Step Inventory for Depression is to focus on personal positives. To force ourselves to realistically identify the personal strengths that have allowed us to stay alive, keep going, and make positive contributions despite our addiction and depression. Our second job is to carefully edit the descriptions of our personal weaknesses. Remove all duplications and exaggerations. This work will prepare you for Step 5.

Another important part of a Fourth Step is to develop a gratitude list, which is a list of all the people and things in our life we are grateful for. When we're locked into the pits of depression, our brain tends to lock onto everything in life that is causing pain and problems. Our depressive brain also tends to block out anything that is going well or giving us pleasure and satisfaction. It's important to fight back against these depressive tendencies by writing a list of things in life that we are grateful for. Let's take a good hard look at what we have and notice the things that are working right, helping us to survive or thrive, and giving us value in our lives. Then let's write these things down on a list and read it to ourselves several times a day to generate some good feelings about the things in our lives that are going well.

Step 5: Sharing the Inventory

> ### Step 5
>
> *Admitted to God, to ourselves, and
> to another human being
> the exact nature of our wrongs.*

Step 5 suggests that we do three things: (1) admit that we're suffering from depression, (2) admit that we're addicted, and (3) admit that we have personal problems or character defects that tend to make our addiction and depression worse. These personal problems, known as *character defects* in Twelve-Step literature, are habitual ways of thinking, managing our feelings, acting, and relating to others in ways that make us uncomfortable in sobriety.

We discovered these defects of character in Step 4. Now, in Step 5, it's suggested that we formally admit and accept responsibility for these problems. This Step suggests that we (1) admit these defects of character to ourselves; (2) affirm our acknowledgment of these character defects to our higher self and Higher Power; and (3) discuss these defects with another person, being as honest as we are able to be about both our strengths and our weaknesses.

We discussed the concept of humility in Step 4. Humble people know who they are in both their strengths and their weaknesses. Step 4 allows us to develop an intellectual understanding of our defects. I call this an "understanding in my head." In order for this knowledge to really help me change, I have to take the "head knowledge" and get it down to the gut level. In other words, I have to carefully reflect on these defects of character and get in touch with both the pain and the pleasure these defects have caused me. The best way to do this is to privately reflect on it when I am alone, pray about it and place the knowledge before my Higher Power, and then discuss it with another person who I can trust to listen and be honest with me.

It is only by confronting yourself in a dialogue with another human being that you can truly come to terms with what has happened to you and who you have become as a result of your addiction and depression. Sharing painful past memories with another caring person—one who will understand what you are saying, take you seriously, and affirm your feelings and experiences as real and valid—provides a sense of relief. You no longer feel alone. You no longer feel like an outcast. You realize that others have had problems similar to yours. You realize that other people can accept you for who you really are. This goes a long way to reduce your feelings of guilt and shame.

Step 6: Willingness to Change

> ### *Step 6*
>
> *Were entirely ready to have God*
> *remove all these defects of character.*

By working Steps 5 and 6 we become consciously aware of our character defects. This allows us to live with a conscious awareness of how these defects affect our day-to-day living. It's only by being aware of the thoughts, feelings, urges, and actions that are motivated by these character defects that we can develop a true willingness to do what's necessary to change. It is by being constantly aware of our character defects and the pain they cause us and those we love that we become willing to give them up. Throughout the process of working Step 6, it is helpful to keep asking for the courage, strength, and means whereby we can grow beyond these defects that follow us into sobriety and contribute to our depression.

Step 7: Asking for Help to Change

> ### Step 7
>
> *Humbly asked our Higher Power to remove our shortcomings.*

In Step 7, we ask our Higher Power to remove the shortcomings and defects of character that contribute to our depression and lead us to relapse. We ask for the ability to recognize what we are thinking, feeling, and doing that is causing unnecessary pain and problems. We also ask for the strength to do what we need to in order to change in ways that will allow us to leave our addiction and depression behind. Our Higher Power gives us the courage and the strength to give up our character defects, but each of us must do the actual giving up. We all must take action and do what the Twelve-Step program calls "the legwork." AA literature constantly points out this dual role—turning to the Higher Power for courage, strength, and hope, and then putting this newfound strength into action. AA members often say it very clearly: "Pray for potatoes but be willing to pick up a hoe and start planting!"

Asking our Higher Power to remove our defects of character which are contributing to our depression and raising our risk of relapse helps us change in important ways on the inside that prepare us for Steps 8 and 9. We get well from the inside out. We must repair ourselves inwardly so we can begin the process of repairing our lives outwardly. First, we recognize the inner habits of mind and emotion that are making us depressed. Only then can we change what we think and feel as a result of these depressive habits. Then we can change how we act. As we behave in a more sober, responsible manner, we become ready to repair the damage our depression and addiction has done to others.

Step 8: Identifying Those We Had Harmed

> ### *Step 8*
>
> *Made a list of all the persons we had harmed and became willing to make amends to them all.*

In Step 8, we come to the realization that our past addictive and depressive behavior has damaged other people. We make a list of the people we have harmed and recognize that we must make an honest attempt to repair the hurt and damage we have caused them. In other words, we must acknowledge that we need to make amends. There is a formula that can help us to remember the critical components of the amends process:

> **Amends = Apology + Changed Behavior + Restitution**

Many recovering people who suffer from depression in sobriety balk at the suggestion that their depression has damaged others: "Even if it did hurt others when I was depressed, I only acted that way when I was depressed so I shouldn't be held responsible." This brings us to an important point: there is a difference between feeling depressed and acting out on the depression in ways that hurt ourselves or others.

Depression is a real illness that interferes with normal emotional functioning. The capacities to feel joy, to relax, and to appropriately respond in an emotional situation are all affected by both abnormal brain chemistry and the presence of depressive beliefs and depressive thinking. This, however, does not give the depressed person the right to use their depression as an excuse for using irresponsible behavior which damages self or others. Just because I feel that life is not worth living and want to kill myself does not mean I have a right to do so. I have a wife, a family, friends, and an important role in my business and community. I have a moral obligation to model, to the best of my ability, a way of coping with the suffering of depression. I may not like it but those are the facts.

As a responsible and conscientious human being, I need to recognize that what I feel is not the same thing as what I do. There is a distinction between what I feel, what I have an urge to do, and what I actually do. I may feel like staying in bed, yet I have the capacity to force myself to get up and get busy. I may feel like spacing out in front of the television, but I have the capacity to force myself to do some other activity that could be more helpful to myself or others. I may feel like isolating myself, but when I realize that my presence is needed by those I love, I can force myself to be present and to get involved. When I force myself to do helpful things despite my depression, the long-term result is that I temporarily become distracted from the depression, I experience some other more pleasant feelings at least for a moment, and I set the stage for instilling new habitual ways of dealing with the depressive feelings that make me better able to manage my depression in the future.

So, in working the steps, I became aware of two important things:

1. *I am not my depression*; and

2. *Just because I feel depressed doesn't mean I need to act out my depression in a way that hurts myself or others.*

These two awarenesses mean that if I did things while depressed that hurt others, and most of us do, I need to acknowledge that to myself and prepare myself to make amends to those people I hurt. I need to recognize that the amends process is a crucial part of my personal recovery from depression because it will free me of the burden of shame and guilt, it will open honest communication between myself and the significant people in my life that I have hurt, and it will strengthen those relationships so they can help me cope more effectively with my depression in the future. Let's take a look at the process of making amends.

Step 9: Making Amends

> ### Step 9
>
> *Made direct amends to such people wherever possible, except when to do so would injure them or others.*

The suggestion made in Step 9 is very clear: we need to make amends to the people we have harmed. We need to make an honest attempt to actually repair the damage that was caused by our addiction and depression if it is within our power to do so. This is the process of "cleaning house" which prepares us for spiritual growth.

So how do we make amends? The amends process starts by developing a strong enough program that will help us maintain sobriety and emotional balance while making amends to others. It is important to remember that a lot of work in recovery must come before the amends process.

The second step is to plan when and how to make amends to each person in an effective manner. Making amends is a serious and difficult process. It is best not to rush into it unprepared. It's important to create a plan. Take the list of people you developed in Step 8 and decide the order in which you will make amends. I recommend starting with the easiest amends processes first so you get some practice before you tackle the more difficult. Decide what you are going to say to each person beforehand and review it with your sponsor and counselor. Then make appointments to talk to each person. Spread out the appointments to make sure you have the time to recuperate from the stress of each conversation. It's important to have the time to reflect on and learn from each experience. One of the goals of making amends is for you to heal on the inside. This takes time and the willingness to talk about the thoughts and feelings that surfaced during each amends session. The amends process, in this sense, is a personal growth experience. But it is more than that. It is also an honest attempt to repair and rebuild a relationship with a person you respect, love, and care about. In that sense, it is an invitation for the other person to forgive you and risk the emotional consequences of trusting you again. This is a process that involves deep feelings, and you need to have quiet time after each experience to listen to what is happening inside of you.

It is important to approach the amends process with an attitude of quiet sincerity. You need to mean what you say, accept responsibility for what you did, and overcome your anger and blaming. This opens you up to feel and express the sorrow and regret over what you have done.

We actually make amends by admitting the reality of our addiction and depression, acknowledging what we did that hurt the other person, taking responsibility for that behavior, and expressing genuine regret for the pain we have caused. Then we pay or make a promise to pay whatever obligations are owed. Sometimes these are financial obligations. Usually, however, the most important obligations are of a personal and emotional nature. The most important payments are usually an offering of respect, kindness, caring, forgiveness, and a genuine desire to rebuild the relationship. The amends process is completed by making a commitment to everything within your power to change in a way that will prevent this kind of damage in the future.

The process of amends is not a guarantee that relationships can be saved. At times they cannot be. There is no rule that says the person with whom you are offering amends needs to accept them. Many won't. By making the genuine offer to repair the damage and rebuild the relationship, you are taking a vital step in releasing the past and gaining knowledge of what you have in the present, so you can move with greater confidence and optimism into the future.

Step 10: Daily Review

> ### *Step 10*
>
> *Continued to take personal inventory and when we were wrong promptly admitted it.*

By the time we reach Step 10 we have made significant progress in our recovery from addiction and depression. In Step 1, we recognized our addiction and depression, acknowledged how these problems had damaged our lives, and became willing to recover. In Step 2, we actively sought a Higher Power who could help us develop the courage, strength, hope, knowledge, and resources to move ahead in our recovery from addiction. In Step 3, we accepted help and became willing to follow suggestions that would guide us in a process of self-change designed to help us to recover. In Step 4, we made an inventory of our strengths and weaknesses so we could develop a greater sense of true humility. In Step 5, we shared this inventory with both our Higher Power and another person, listening carefully to what they had to say in response and became willing to learn from it. In Step 6, we became willing to change, and in Step 7, we let our ego get out of the way and allowed the change process to work in a natural way within us. In Step 8, we turned our attention outward to the people we harmed by our addictive and depressive behaviors. In Step 9, we made direct amends. If these

Steps are done with any degree of thoroughness, a new consciousness begins to develop. A new view of ourselves and our life begins to emerge. In Step 10, we protect our newly found recovery.

Step 10 suggests that we take a personal inventory every day and when we are wrong promptly admit it. Many people suffering from depression have found that a slight addition to this step is beneficial—to inventory the things we are doing right as well as the things we are doing wrong. Depressed people tend to be pessimistic and look for reasons to give up hope. Therefore, it's important that our daily inventory focus on teaching us to catch ourselves doing things right and celebrating that as well as catching ourselves doing things wrong and making corrections to get us back on track.

I once knew a commercial airline pilot who was in recovery. After a meeting in which we discussed the Tenth Step, he posed a riddle: "How much of the time is a jet liner exactly on course as it flies from New York to California." My answer was most of the time. The recovering pilot corrected me. "The commercial airliner is off course 98 percent of the time. So as pilots we're constantly making mid-course corrections to compensate for wind and weather patterns. It's only essential that we're exactly on course at two critical moments—when we take off and when we land." The Tenth Step is the process we all use to make mid-course corrections as we navigate the journey of our lives.

Step 11: Conscious Contact with Our Higher Power

> ### Step 11
>
> *Sought through prayer and meditation to improve our conscious contact with God as we understood Him, praying only for knowledge of His will for us and the power to carry that out.*

If you have been reading carefully and reflecting deeply on the ideas we've been considering, you may begin to notice a feeling stirring deep within you. This feeling may be a sense of quiet power. It may be the sense of being connected to something bigger than yourself. It may come from the awareness that you are reflecting on principles and practices that have been seriously considered by all intelligent people of goodwill since the beginning of human civilization. This feeling is a sense that we are not alone, that we are never alone. It is the knowledge that we always have available to us this center of quiet strength that will give us the courage and hope to do what we have to do. Out of this collective consciousness of our spiritual traditions has come a series of simple steps that help us to know what we need to do to connect with this quiet sense of power.

We have now entered the realm of spirituality. This is the realm of conscious contact with our Higher Power. This is the personal realm in which we must make a decision about two different approaches to the concept of a Higher Power. We must either acknowledge that a Higher Power exists and seek to become more closely connected with that Power or we run from that knowledge and that experience. If you choose to experiment with building your conscious relationship with your Higher Power, Step 11 is the Step for you.

Addiction and depression usually damage, distort, or destroy our spiritual values. By *spiritual,* I mean the nonphysical aspect of our being—our thoughts, feelings, attitudes, values, and beliefs. As we clear the wreckage from our past, we can at last experience a new sense of spiritual freedom. We can contact the psychic energy or life force within us in new and exciting ways. You can learn to become still and listen to that quiet, yet powerful voice within you that connects with the true values of life. In AA terms, we can develop a conscious contact with the God of our understanding—our Higher Power.

Step 12: Carrying the Message

> ### *Step 12*
>
> *Having had a spiritual awakening as a result of these steps, we tried to carry this message to other people suffering from addiction and depression, and to practice these principles in all our affairs.*

What AA calls a "spiritual awakening" is a radical transformation or change in perception, attitude, and personality. You begin to feel changed because you are thinking differently, managing your feelings differently, acting differently, and relating to others in a different way. Most importantly, you have made a commitment to persist in using these new ways of thinking, feeling, acting, and relating to others whether you feel like it or not. As a result of this step, you have made a decision and developed a capacity to somehow rise above the addictive and depressive program that has hijacked your brain. You have come to realize that you are not your addictive or depressive thoughts—you are the thinker of those thoughts. You are not what you feel—you are the spiritual consciousness that is aware of your feelings. You are not what you do—you are the doer. You are not your relationship—you are the person who chooses to relate. As a result, you can change what you think, how you manage your feelings, what you do, and how you relate to people. By making these changes you will become aware of a new self—a higher self that is capable of connecting with the quiet strength of your Higher Power working within you and through you.

The Higher Self Meditation

I am not my addictive or depressive thoughts—
    I am the thinker of those thoughts.
I am not what I feel—
    I am the spiritual consciousness
    that is aware of my feelings.
I am not what I do—
    I am the doer.
I am not my relationships—
    I am the person who chooses to relate.
Therefore I can change these things
    and still be me!

The Steps change us in subtle and profound ways. Because of these changes we are ready to go out and carry the message of what we have learned and experienced to other recovering people. It is important to remember that Step 12 also instructs us to keep practicing Twelve-Step principles in all our affairs. Thus, working the Twelve-Step program never really ends.

Those are the Twelve Steps in a nutshell. This overview provides a shorthand version for understanding how the Twelve Steps can be applied to recovery from both addiction and depression. If this approach to recovery appeals to you, more information on the Steps is readily available. Please refer to Appendix 6, which provides recommended reading on the Twelve-Step program.

Appendix 1: Depression Evaluation Questionnaire

Answer each question by placing a check in the box in front of the correct answer

$$1 \quad 2 \quad 3 \quad 4 \quad 5 \quad 6 \quad 7 \quad 8 \quad 9 \quad 10$$

⟵————————————————————⟶

1-1. How Depressed Are You?

❏ 1–3 = When I get depressed, my depression is a nuisance but I can always function normally with extra effort.

❏ 5–9 = When I get depressed, at times I can function normally with extra effort and at other times I can't.

❏ 10 = When I get depressed, I usually cannot function normally even with extra effort.

1	2	3	4	5	6	7	8	9	10

←—————————————————————————————————→

1-2. How often do you feel depressed?

❑ 1 = Almost Never

❑ 5 = About half of the time

❑ 10 = Almost all of the time

1-3. How long does each episode of depression last?

❑ 1 = Less than an hour

❑ 5 = Several days

❑ 10 = I'm depressed all of the time with no break between episodes.

1–4. How severe are the negative consequences that your depression causes?

❑ 1 = Mild: I feel bad but there are no negative consequences.

❑ 5 = Moderate: My depression causes some serious problems in my life.

❑ 10 = Severe: My depression causes serious damage to my health, emotional well-being, and lifestyle.

1-5. Has your depression made you think about dying or killing yourself?

(This is called a suicide check and it's important for all depressed people to consciously review these questions on a regular basis.)

1. I sometimes feel that life isn't worth living.
    ❑ Yes   ❑ No   ❑ Unsure

2. I sometimes think I would be better off dead.
    ❑ Yes   ❑ No   ❑ Unsure

3. I sometimes think about killing myself.
  ❏ Yes   ❏ No   ❏ Unsure

4. I sometimes think about the things I could do to kill myself.
  ❏ Yes   ❏ No   ❏ Unsure

5. I have developed a plan to kill myself.
  ❏ Yes   ❏ No   ❏ Unsure

6. I have everything I need to carry out the plan.
  ❏ Yes   ❏ No   ❏ Unsure

7. I have tried to kill myself in the past.
      Yes   No   Unsure

8. I will probably try to kill myself sometime in the future.
  ❏ Yes   ❏ No   ❏ Unsure

9. I have strong and compelling reasons for staying alive that will keep me from trying to hurt myself.
  ❏ Yes   ❏ No   ❏ Unsure

Note: If you answer "yes" to questions 3, 4, 5, 6, or 8 you are so seriously depressed that you need to seek professional help immediately.

Appendix 2: Suicidal Thoughts Questionnaire— Long Form

Appendix 2: Suicidal Thoughts Questionnaire—Long Form:	
Instructions: Read each statement. Think about how often you tend to think that thought and how you feel when you're thinking it. Then answer the questions listed under each thought.	

1. Life isn't worth living.	
A. *How often do you tend to think this thought?*	Very Often Often Seldom Almost Never
B. *When this thought comes to mind, how convinced are you that it's true?*	Very Convinced Convinced Doubtful Very Doubtful
C. *How does this thought affect your depression?*	Makes it worse Makes it better Has no noticeable affect
D. *When this thought comes to mind, how often do you try to think other thoughts that will make you feel better?*	Very Often Often Seldom Almost Never

E.	How often do you try to convince yourself that this thought is not true and force yourself to think other thoughts that will make you feel better?	Very Often Often Seldom Almost Never
2.	**I would be better off dead.**	
A.	How often do you tend to think this thought?	Very Often Often Seldom Almost Never
B.	When this thought comes to mind, how convinced are you that it's true?	Very Convinced Convinced Doubtful Very Doubtful
C.	How does this thought affect your depression?	Makes it worse Makes it better Has no noticeable affect
D.	When this thought comes to mind, how often do you try to think other thoughts that will make you feel better?	Very Often Often Seldom Almost Never
E.	How often do you try to convince yourself that this thought is not true and force yourself to think other thoughts that will make you feel better?	Very Often Often Seldom Almost Never
3.	**I sometimes think about killing myself.**	
A.	How often do you tend to think this thought?	Very Often Often Seldom Almost Never
B.	When this thought comes to mind, how convinced are you that it's true?	Very Convinced Convinced Doubtful Very Doubtful
C.	How does this thought affect your depression?	Makes it worse Makes it better Has no noticeable affect
D.	When this thought comes to mind, how often do you try to think other thoughts that will make you feel better?	Very Often Often Seldom Almost Never
E.	How often do you try to convince yourself that this thought is not true and force yourself to think other thoughts that will make you feel better?	Very Often Often Seldom Almost Never

4.	**I sometimes think about ways to kill myself.**		
	A.	*How often do you tend to think this thought?*	Very Often Often Seldom Almost Never
	B.	*When this thought comes to mind, how convinced are you that it's true?*	Very Convinced Convinced Doubtful Very Doubtful
	C.	*How does this thought affect your depression?*	Makes it worse Makes it better Has no noticeable affect
	D.	*When this thought comes to mind, how often do you try to think other thoughts that will make you feel better?*	Very Often Often Seldom Almost Never
	E.	*How often do you try to convince yourself that this thought is not true and force yourself to think other thoughts that will make you feel better?*	Very Often Often Seldom Almost Never
5.	**I have a plan to kill myself.**		
	A.	*How often do you tend to think this thought?*	Very Often Often Seldom Almost Never
	B.	*When this thought comes to mind, how convinced are you that it's true?*	Very Convinced Convinced Doubtful Very Doubtful
	C.	*How does this thought affect your depression?*	Makes it worse Makes it better Has no noticeable affect
	D.	*When this thought comes to mind, how often do you try to think other thoughts that will make you feel better?*	Very Often Often Seldom Almost Never
	E.	*How often do you try to convince yourself that this thought is not true and force yourself to think other thoughts that will make you feel better?*	Very Often Often Seldom Almost Never

6.	I have everything I need to carry out the plan.	
	A. How often do you tend to think this thought?	Very Often Often Seldom Almost Never
	B. When this thought comes to mind, how convinced are you that it's true?	Very Convinced Convinced Doubtful Very Doubtful
	C. How does this thought affect your depression?	Makes it worse Makes it better Has no noticeable affect
	D. When this thought comes to mind, how often do you try to think other thoughts that will make you feel better?	Very Often Often Seldom Almost Never
	E. How often do you try to convince yourself that this thought is not true and force yourself to think other thoughts that will make you feel better?	Very Often Often Seldom Almost Never
7.	I have tried to kill myself in the past.	
	A. How often do you tend to think this thought?	Very Often Often Seldom Almost Never
	B. When this thought comes to mind, how convinced are you that it's true?	Very Convinced Convinced Doubtful Very Doubtful
	C. How does this thought affect your depression?	Makes it worse Makes it better Has no noticeable affect
	D. When this thought comes to mind, how often do you try to think other thoughts that will make you feel better?	Very Often Often Seldom Almost Never
	E. How often do you try to convince yourself that this thought is not true and force yourself to think other thoughts that will make you feel better?	Very Often Often Seldom Almost Never

8.	**I will probably try to kill myself sometime in the future.**	
	A. How often do you tend to think this thought?	Very Often Often Seldom Almost Never
	B. When this thought comes to mind, how convinced are you that it's true?	Very Convinced Convinced Doubtful Very Doubtful
	C. How does this thought affect your depression?	Makes it worse Makes it better Has no noticeable affect
	D. When this thought comes to mind, how often do you try to think other thoughts that will make you feel better?	Very Often Often Seldom Almost Never
	E. How often do you try to convince yourself that this thought is not true and force yourself to think other thoughts that will make you feel better?	Very Often Often Seldom Almost Never
9.	**I have strong and compelling reasons for staying alive that will keep me from trying to hurt myself.**	
	A. How often do you tend to think this thought?	Very Often Often Seldom Almost Never
	B. When this thought comes to mind, how convinced are you that it's true?	Very Convinced Convinced Doubtful Very Doubtful
	C. How does this thought affect your depression?	Makes it worse Makes it better Has no noticeable affect
	D. When this thought comes to mind, how often do you try to think other thoughts that will make you feel better?	Very Often Often Seldom Almost Never
	E. How often do you try to convince yourself that this thought is not true and force yourself to think other thoughts that will make you feel better?	Very Often Often Seldom Almost Never

Suicidal Thoughts Questionnaire— Short Form

1. I sometimes feel that life isn't worth living.
   ❏ Yes   ❏ No   ❏ Unsure

2. I sometimes think I would be better off dead.
   ❏ Yes   ❏ No   ❏ Unsure

3. I sometimes think about killing myself.
   ❏ Yes   ❏ No   ❏ Unsure

4. I sometimes think about ways of killing myself.
   ❏ Yes   ❏ No   ❏ Unsure

5. I have developed a plan to kill myself.
   ❏ Yes   ❏ No   ❏ Unsure

6. I have everything I need to carry out the plan.

❑   Yes   ❑ No   ❑ Unsure

7. I have tried to kill myself in the past.

❑   Yes   ❑ No   ❑ Unsure

8. I will probably try to kill myself sometime in the future.

❑   Yes   ❑ No   ❑ Unsure

9. I have strong and compelling reasons for staying alive that will keep me from trying to hurt myself.

❑   Yes   ❑ No   ❑ Unsure

Note: If you answer "yes" to questions 3, 4, 5, 6, or 8 you are so seriously depressed that you need to seek professional help immediately.

Appendix 3: How to Encourage a Depressed Person to Get Help

Here are some guidelines for how to encourage people who are suffering from depression to get the help they need. Ultimately it is the responsibility of the depressed person to seek help, but effective communication, accurate information, and appropriate support can help them get the correct help sooner.

1. **Talk to the depressed person and honestly report what you are seeing:** Recovery from addiction or any other mental health problem is based on a program of rigorous honesty. You have to know the truth about what is happening, name the truth, and talk about it openly and nonjudgmentally. When you're in a relationship with a depressed person in recovery from addiction, the natural tendency is to stay away from them, leave them alone, and try to protect them from the reality of what is going on.

This is called enabling. You may do this with the best of intentions, but the result will be to participate in the person's addiction and depression by pretending that it doesn't exist. This just lengthens the amount of time it takes for all involved to recognize the problems, understand what is happening, explore resources for treatment and recovery, and develop a cooperative way to help everyone involved to deal with the depression, addiction, and related problems.

2. **Help the depressed person get help:** The most important thing anyone can do for the depressed person is to help him or her get an appropriate diagnosis and treatment. This means that you need to recognize that the person is depressed, open communication with them in a supportive and honest way, and encourage him or her to get help. Remember, depression is a disease of pessimism and hopelessness. It's important for you to be realistic yet hopeful and optimistic that if the right things are done, the depression can get better and related problems can be solved.

If your friend or family member is already in treatment, get involved. Have a session with the therapist, research and discuss the medication the person is on, and offer to become part of the treatment and recovery plan. This may involve encouraging the individual to stay with treatment until symptoms begin to abate (several weeks), or to seek different treatment if no improvement occurs. On occasion, it may require making an appointment and accompanying the depressed person to the doctor and telling the therapist or doctor what you are seeing in terms of the depression, addiction, and related problems. This is especially important if you know the depressed person is thinking about or talking about suicide.

You should encourage the depressed person to follow the doctor's orders and follow the treatment plan they developed with their therapist. You need to be careful, however, not to allow the depressed person to shift the responsibility for their recovery onto you. You can't treat their depression or addiction. You can simply stay involved, support the person, and tell the truth about what you see happening and offer to help in ways that are acceptable to you.

The second most important thing is to offer emotional support. This involves understanding, patience, affection, and encouragement. Engage the depressed person in conversation and listen carefully. Do not disparage feelings expressed, but point out realities and offer hope. Do not ignore remarks about suicide. Report them to the depressed person's therapist. Invite the depressed person for walks, outings, to the movies, and other activities. Be gently insistent if your invitation is refused. Encourage participation in some activities that once gave pleasure, such as hobbies, sports, or religious or cultural activities, but do not push the depressed person to undertake too much too soon. The depressed person needs diversion and company, but too many demands can increase feelings of failure.

3. **Offer emotional support:** The most important thing depressed people need is to know that other people still love and care about them. Try to find some common interests. Tell them you care. Offer to sit and listen. Just be with them and let them know you'll do your best to be there for them.

4. **Don't accuse the depressed person of faking illness or of laziness:** Depression may appear as laziness. The person may feel and act sick and go

to a doctor who finds nothing wrong with them. They may even start in therapy or begin using medication with little or no results. It's easy to assume that the person is faking their depression to get out of performing responsibilities or holding up their end of the relationship. If the person is suffering from a depressive illness, this isn't true.

For people with a history of working hard and being responsible, the depression can hit doubly hard. In such cases, the depressed person may feel lazy, irresponsible, and incompetent because they can't do what they used to be able to do. This can attack their feeling of self-worth, undermine their self-confidence, and make them feel guilty and ashamed. They may believe they should just be able to snap out of it and behave like normal. When they can't they tend to be very hard on themselves and start feeling embarrassed, guilty, and ashamed. These feelings may motivate them to want to hide their depression, to stay away from others when the symptoms are at their worst, and only deal with others when they can fake it for a while and pretend everything is OK.

5. **Don't expect the depressed person to "snap out of it":** People don't suddenly and dramatically recover from depression. It's a long, slow process with numerous ups and downs. It's important to be realistic and encourage the depressed person to maintain their treatment and recovery program even when it seems like things aren't working at the moment. Recovery involves consistency. Eventually, with proper treatment and an effective recovery plan, most people do get better. Keep that in mind, and keep reassuring the depressed person that, with time and help, he or she will feel better.

Appendix 4: Talking with Someone Who Is Suicidal

http://www.metanoia.org/suicide/sphone.htm

Just about everyone who feels suicidal will try to talk about it with someone. The attempt may be feeble and indirect, but the effort will be made. The way other people respond to someone who is feeling suicidal makes a great deal of difference.

When a suicidal person tells you about their feelings of wanting to die and believing that life isn't worth living, they are asking you to help them find a way to fight back against these feelings. They are reaching out for help and seeking a source of courage, strength, and hope so they can carry on. So, at these important moments when people turn to us for help, what can we do? Here are my suggestions:

1. **Recognize that something important is happening.** Sometimes it's hard to believe that the person we're talking with is really thinking about killing himself or herself. There is a tendency to rationalize, deny, and shut down the conversation. So it's important for us to stop and realize this is a serious request for help and how we respond can and will make a difference.

2. **Be yourself.** Don't try to become a therapist or counselor. Don't feel you have to say the right words. Just let yourself feel your concern and let the person know you care and you are interested in listening to what he or she has to say.

3. **Let the person talk.** This can be hard. We often feel we must say or do something to save the person. The most important thing you can do is get the person talking, listen to them in a caring and accepting way, and empathize with what they are thinking and feeling.

4. **Listen to what the person is saying.** The first thing is to hear the words and respond. Active listening is helpful. Active listening is a communication technique that helps others feel listened to, understood, and taken seriously. To use active listening, here's what you do. First, listen to what the person says. Then tell the person what you heard them say. It's often best to use the same words the person said to you. If, for example, the person says, "I feel so bad I don't know if I can handle it anymore," you could respond by saying something like the following: "Wow! What I'm hearing you say is that things are really tough right now and you're not sure you can handle it. Did I hear you correctly?" If the person says yes, then ask them to tell you more about it. If they say

that you didn't hear them correctly, explain that you really want to understand them and to tell you again. This approach usually makes it easy for a conversation to begin and continue.

5. **Let the person vent their thoughts and feelings.** Once they start talking, encourage them to keep going. Don't interrupt. Don't try to set them straight or give advice. Just let them talk, tell them what you are hearing them say, and let them know that it's OK to talk about it. The person may talk about feeling helpless and hopeless. They may tell you they are in a state of despair and believe that nothing will ever get any betterr. They may start to express anger and tell you about all the things that are going wrong.

6. **Remember, the person needs to talk.** Just telling you about these things usually makes the person feel better. If you listen in a caring way, you can become a source of strength and hope to help them get through the moment. No matter how bad the things are that the person tells you about remember this: Getting it out will relieve the pressure. This is a cry for help, and by listening you are giving them the help they need.

7. **Be sympathetic, nonjudgmental, patient, calm, and accepting.** Let the person know they have done the right thing by talking to you. Say something like this: "I know you're feeling really bad, but you're doing the right thing by talking to me about this. No matter how bad things may seem, it's not helpless. By talking these things through with me and with other people you can find a way to get through this."

8. **Don't be afraid to use the "S" word.** The "S" word, of course, is SUICIDE. If the person says

something like, "Things are so bad, I'm not sure I can go on," ask the "S" Question: "Have you thought about suicide? Have things gotten so bad that you've thought you'd be better off dead?" Sometimes it's easier to work up to it with a series of three questions: (1) Do you sometimes feel that life isn't worth living? (2) Do you sometimes feel that you would be better off dead? (3) Have you ever thought about killing yourself?

Don't be afraid of putting ideas in their head. People don't start thinking about killing themselves just because you ask them about it. Asking the suicide question is the right thing to do. You're showing the person that you're concerned, that you're sharp enough to recognize what's going on, and, most importantly, that your're not afraid to talk about it. You're giving them the clear message that it's OK for the person to share his or her pain with you.

What if the person says "yes"? You go to the next step and ask them some more questions. Here's another series of questions that are helpful: (1) Have you thought about how you will kill yourself? Have you developed a plan? (2) Do you think that you might try to kill yourself in the future? (3) Do you have what you need to carry out the plan? (4) Have you decided when and where you will do it? (5) Have you ever tried to kill yourself in the past? What did you do to get the help you needed to get through the crisis then?

Most people, at some point, will start saying "no" to some of these questions. This will be a relief for both you and the person you are talking to. If someone has a plan, a time, and place selected it is an emergency. Get the person emergency help. If they refuse, call "911" or the police.

Just talking about their feelings and letting them know that you are concerned will give suicidal people relief from loneliness and pent-up feelings. It will show them that another person cares, is willing to listen to them, and understands what's going on. Talking about depression and suicidal thoughts causes a change in feeling and physical release of stress and tension. These conversations actually change brain chemistry in a way that allows the body to release stress and tension. The sense of relief that follows can take the edge off their feelings, give them a sense of relief, and give them enough hope to get through a bad moment.

9. **Let the person know that this, too, will pass.** Say something like, "I can see how bad you're feeling, but I know this: If you can just hang on for a while, things will start to feel better." Ask the person if they've ever felt this bad and gotten through it. Ask them what they did.

10. **Explain that people feel suicidal when pain gets so bad they can't stand it and they lack the ability to cope with the pain.** We can always find ways to reduce our pain. We can do something to make ourselves feel a little bit better. We can also do things to help us cope more effectively with the pain and get through the hard times.

11. **There are some things you shouldn't do.** Avoid arguments. Don't try to identify, clarify, and resolve problems. This can be overwhelming and there will be time to deal with reality later. Don't give advice. Nobody likes being told what to do, especially if you're feeling so depressed you don't believe you

can do it. Don't tell the person you know how they're feeling—you don't. Even if you do, the person won't believe you because their feelings are so strong and so personal, they don't believe anyone could be feeling the same way. Don't say anything that will make the person feel guilty or ashamed for feeling suicidal. It is not how bad the problem is, but how badly it's hurting the person who has it.

12. **If the person is drinking or using drugs, they can be at special risk.** Alcohol and drugs impair judgment and impulse control. The person is more likely to make a bad choice and will be less likely to fight back against suicidal feelings. If someone is drinking or drugging, you need to think about getting the person to professional help. Don't forget "911" and the police.

13. **Whenever talking to someone who feels suicidal, be sure you know how to contact them and significant others in their lives.** Get their address and phone number. Ask for the name and phone number of their spouse, friend, or Twelve-Step sponsor.

14. **Recognize your limits.** You don't have the power to save anyone. All you can do is respond in a genuine, caring way when someone reaches out to you and point them in the direction to get help. You can't control what will happen. The most important thing you can do is recommend that the person get in touch with a trained addiction and mental-health professional. Anyone who feels suicidal should get professional help, and the sooner the better.

15. **Don't keep secrets.** Many depressed and suicidal people will invite you into a secrets game. It goes like this: "I have something very serious to

tell you, but I'll only tell you if you promise not to tell anyone else." My rule is to always tell the person that I can't agree: "If you tell me something that leads me to believe that you need help, I'm going to do whatever I have to do to get you the help you need. If that's not OK, don't tell me. Go talk with someone else."

Warning Signs:

- Conditions associated with increased risk of suicide
- Death or terminal illness of relative or friend
- Divorce, separation, broken relationship, stress on family
- Loss of health (real or imaginary)
- Loss of job, home, money, status, self-esteem, personal security
- Alcohol or drug abuse

Depression

In the young, depression may be masked by hyperactivity or acting-out behavior. In the elderly, it may be incorrectly attributed to the natural effects of aging. Depression that seems to quickly disappear for no apparent reason is cause for concern. The early stages of recovery from depression can be a high-risk period. Recent studies have associated anxiety disorders with increased risk for attempted suicide.

Emotional and behavioral changes associated with suicide

- Overwhelming pain: pain that threatens to exceed the person's pain-coping capacities. Suicidal feelings are often the result of long-standing problems that have been exacerbated by recent precipitating events. The precipitating factors may be new pain or the loss of pain-coping resources.

- Hopelessness: the feeling that the pain will continue or get worse; things will never get better.

- Powerlessness: the feeling that one's resources for reducing pain are exhausted.

- Feelings of worthlessness, shame, guilt, self-hatred, "no one cares." Fears of losing control, harming self or others.

- Personality becomes sad, withdrawn, tired, apathetic, anxious, irritable, or prone to angry outbursts.

- Declining performance in school, work, or other activities. (Occasionally the reverse: someone who volunteers for extra duties because they need to fill up their time.)

- Social isolation, or association with a group that has different moral standards than those of the family.

- Declining interest in sex, friends, or activities previously enjoyed.

- Neglect of personal welfare, deteriorating physical appearance.

- Alterations in either direction of sleeping or eating habits.

- (Particularly in the elderly) Self-starvation, dietary mismanagement, disobeying medical instructions.

- Difficult times: holidays, anniversaries, and the first week after discharge from a hospital; just before and after diagnosis of a major illness; just before and during disciplinary proceedings. Undocumented status adds to the stress of a crisis.

- Suicidal behavior

- Previous suicide attempts, "mini-attempts."

- Explicit statements of suicidal ideation or feelings.

- Development of suicidal plan, acquiring the means, "rehearsal" behavior, setting a time for the attempt.

- Self-inflicted injuries, such as cuts, burns, or head banging.

- Reckless behavior. (Besides suicide, other leading causes of death among young people in New York City are homicide, accidents, drug overdose, and AIDS.) Unexplained accidents among children and the elderly.

- Making out a will or giving away favorite possessions.

- Inappropriately saying goodbye.

- Verbal behavior that is ambiguous or indirect: "I'm going away on a real long trip," "You won't have to worry about me anymore," "I want to go to sleep and never wake up," "I'm so depressed, I just can't go on," "Does God punish suicides?" "Voices are telling me to do bad things"; requests for euthanasia information, inappropriate joking, stories or essays on morbid themes.

A Warning about Warning Signs

The majority of the population at any one time does not have many of the warning signs and has a lower suicide risk rate. But a lower rate in a larger population is still a lot of people—and many completed suicides had only a few of the conditions listed above. In a one-person-to-another-person situation, all indications of suicidality need to be taken seriously.

Crisis-intervention hotlines that accept calls from the suicidal, or anyone who wishes to discuss a problem, are (in New York City) (212) 673-3000 and Helpline at (212) 532-2400.

If unsure where to go for help, check the Yellow Pages under "mental health," "health," "social services," "suicide prevention," "crisis-intervention services," "hotlines," "hospitals," or "physicians" for phone numbers and addresses. In times of crisis, the emergency room doctor at a hospital may be able to provide only temporary help for an emotional problem, and will be able to tell you where and how to get further help.

Appendix 5: Where to Get Help

Here is a list of the types of people and places that will make a referral to, or provide, diagnostic and treatment services:

1. Family doctors
2. Mental-health specialists, such as psychiatrists, psychologists, social workers, or mental health counselors
3. Health-maintenance organizations
4. Community mental-health centers
5. Hospital psychiatry departments and outpatient clinics
6. University- or medical school-affiliated programs
7. State hospital outpatient clinics
8. Family service, social agencies, or clergy
9. Private clinics and facilities

10. Employee-assistance programs
11. Local medical and/or psychiatric societies

Appendix 6: For Further Information on Depression

1. National Institute of Mental Health Information Resources and Inquiries Branch

6001 Executive Boulevard
Room 8184, MSC 9663
Bethesda, MD 20892-9663
Telephone: (301) 443-4513
FAX: (301) 443-4279
TTY: (301) 443-8431
FAX4U: (301) 443-5158
Web site: *http://www.nimh.nih.gov*
E-mail: *nimhinfo@nih.gov*

2. National Alliance for the Mentally Ill (NAMI)
Colonial Place Three

2107 Wilson Blvd., Suite 300
Arlington, VA 22201
Phone: 1-800-950-NAMI (6264); or (703) 524-7600
Web site: *http://www.nami.org*

Description: A support and advocacy organization of consumers, families, and friends of people with severe mental illness—more than 1,200 state and local affiliates. Local affiliates often give guidance in finding treatment.

3. Depression and Bipolar Support Alliance (DBSA)

730 N. Franklin St., Suite #501,
Chicago, IL 60610-7204
Telephone: (312) 988-1150
Fax: (312) 642-7243
Web site: *www.DBSAlliance.org*

Description: The purpose of DBSA is to educate patients, families, and the public concerning the nature of depressive illnesses. DBSA maintains an extensive catalog of helpful books.

4. National Foundation for Depressive Illness, Inc.

P.O. Box 2257
New York, NY 10116
Telephone: (212) 268-4260; or 1-800-239-1265
Web site: *http://www.depression.org*

Description: The National Foundation for Depressive Illness, Inc. is a foundation that informs the public about depressive illness and its treatability and promotes programs of research, education, and treatment.

5. National Mental Health Association (NMHA)
2001 N. Beauregard Street, 12th Floor
Alexandria, VA 22311
Telephone: 1-800-969-6942; or (703) 684-7722
TTY: 1-800-443-5959
Web site: *http://www.nmha.org*

Description: NMHA is an association that works with 340 affiliates to promote mental health through advocacy, education, research, and services.

Glossary

addiction: a chronic, relapsing disease, characterized by compulsive drug-seeking and drug use and by neurochemical and molecular changes in the brain.

analog: a chemical compound that is similar to another drug in its effects but differs slightly in its chemical structure.

benzodiazepines : drugs that relieve anxiety or are prescribed as sedatives; among the most widely prescribed medications, including Valium® and Librium®.

central nervous system (CNS): the brain and spinal cord.

craving: a powerful, often uncontrollable desire for drugs.

depressed mood: A depressed mood occurs when a person experiences a limited period of low energy, lethargy, and loss of motivation. A depressed mood differs from depression in severity, duration, and consequences. A depressed mood is less severe, shorter in duration, and has no serious consequences because it does not interfere with the ability to maintain normal acts of daily living.

depression: Depression occurs when a depressed mood becomes so severe that it interferes with normal acts of daily living (i.e., normal daily routines necessary to maintain interpersonal relationships, work activities, or the maintenance tasks of life) it is called *depression*. Depression differs from depressed mood in severity, duration, and consequences. Depression is more severe, longer in duration, and has serious consequences because it interferes with the ability to maintain normal acts of daily living.

designer drug: an analog of a restricted drug that has psychoactive properties.

detoxification : a process of allowing the body to rid itself of a drug while managing the symptoms of withdrawal; often the first step in a drug treatment program.

dopamine: a neurotransmitter present in regions of the brain that regulates movement, emotion, motivation, and feelings of pleasure.

dysthymia: a chronic, long-term, low-grade depression. People with dysthymia feel like they are living in a state of chronic, low-grade emergency. They feel bad enough to know that something is wrong, but they usually don't feel bad enough to seek help.

futility: A feeling commonly experienced by depressed people that is based on the mistaken belief that "No matter what I do, it won't help—there is no one and nothing that can ever help me."

helplessness: A feeling commonly experienced by depressed people that is based on the mistaken belief that "There is nothing I can do!" This mistaken belief can be challenged by using self-talk like this: "There is always something that can be done to make things a little bit better. I may be having a bad day, but this, too, will pass."

hopelessness: A feeling commonly experienced by depressed people that is based on the mistaken belief that "Nothing can or will ever be different."

hypersomnia: A symptom of depression (included in DSM-IV-TR Major Depressive Episode—Criterion 4) that includes sleeping too much, sleeping for extremely long periods of time, inability to awaken and become active in the morning or when you have important activities to complete, and feeling constantly tired and fatigued despite sleeping a lot.

inner dialogue: Inner dialogue is a conversation we have in the privacy of our mind. We create different characters in our own mind who take on different sides of an argument or debate. Inner dialogues allow us to give a voice to all sides of an issue and work through a process that produces a deeper level of understanding. Inner dialogue, like self-talk, can be automatic and unconscious or it can be consciously self-regulated.

insomnia: A symptom of depression (included in DSM-IV-TR Major Depressive Episode—Criterion 4) that includes having difficulty falling asleep, staying asleep throughout the night, or waking up in the early morning without feeling rested.

mania: When a stimulated mood becomes so severe that it interferes with normal acts of daily living, it is called *mania*. When a person swings between severely depressed moods and extremely stimulated moods, it is called *manic depression*. This manic-depressive continuum becomes a vital tool in recognizing normal mood swings and distinguishing them from mood disorders.

narcolepsy: a disorder characterized by uncontrollable attacks of deep sleep.

physical dependence: an adaptive physiological state that occurs with regular drug use and results in a withdrawal syndrome when drug use stops.

psychosis: a mental disorder characterized by symptoms such as delusions or hallucinations that indicate an impaired conception of reality.

relapse-prone person: someone who recognizes that they're addicted and makes a sincere attempt to stop using alcohol and other drugs by using a combination of professional treatment and self-help programs. But they return to drinking and drug use despite their commitment to stay sober. Just as no one is immune from the disease of addiction, few people are immune from depression.

resiliency: the ability to bounce back from adversity. Resilient people are able to deal with high levels of stress and disappointment without becoming depressed. Resilient people usually have physical, psychological, and social protective skills that allow them to bounce back from adversity.

rush: a surge of euphoric pleasure that rapidly follows administration of a drug.

secondary gains: the positive things that your problems or illnesses are doing for you.

self-talk: the process of talking to yourself in the privacy of your own mind. Self-talk can be consciously self-regulated or it can become automatic and unconscious. A thought just pops into your mind.

serotonin: a neurotransmitter that has been implicated in states of consciousness, mood, depression, and anxiety.

tolerance: a condition in which higher doses of a drug are required to produce the same effect as experienced initially; often leads to physical dependence.

toxic: temporary or permanent drug effects that are detrimental to the functioning of an organ or group of organs.

withdrawal : a variety of symptoms that occurs after use of an addictive drug is reduced or stopped.

Bibliography

Ban, T.A. "Pharmacotherapy of Depression: A Historical Analysis," Vanderbilt University, Nashville, Tennessee. *J Neural Transm* 108, no. 6 (2001): 707–716; on the Internet: *http://www .biopsychiatry.com/history.html*

Beck, Aaron T. *The Diagnosis and Management of Depression.* Philadelphia: University of Pennsylvania Press, 1973.

Beck, Aaron T. et al. *Cognitive Therapy of Depression*, New York: Guilford Press, 1979.

Beasley, C. "Activation and Sedation in Fluoxetine Clinical Studies"; unpublished in-house document generated by Eli Lilly and Company during the FDA-approval process of Prozac for depression and obtained during discovery for Fentress v. Shay Communications et al., Fentress Trial Exhibit 70, 1988.

Blehar, M.D. and D.A. Oren. "Gender Differences in Depression," *Medscape Women's Health* 2 (1997): 3; revised from "Women's Increased Vulnerability to Mood Disorders: Integrating Psychobiology and Epidemiology," *Depression* 3 (1995): 3–12.

Breggin, Peter R. "Suicidality, Violence and Mania Caused by Selective Serotonin Reuptake Inhibitors (SSRIs): A Review and Analysis," *International Journal of Risk & Safety in Medicine* 16 (2003/2004): 31–49.

_____. *Brain-Disabling Treatments in Psychiatry: Drugs, Electroshock, and the Role of the FDA.* New York: Springer, 1997.

_____. "Testimony in Joyce Fentress et al. vs. Shea Communications et al." [The Wesbecker Case]. Jefferson Circuit Court, Division, 1, Louisville, Kentucky, No. 90-CI-06033, Volume XVI, 1994.

DePaulo, J. Raymond. *Understanding Depression: What We Know and What We Can Do About It.* Hoboken, New Jersey: John Wiley and Sons, 2002.

Dufour, Mary C. "What Is Moderate Drinking? Defining 'Drinks' and Drinking Levels," *Alcohol & Health* 23, no. 1 (1999).

Fentress et al. vs. Shea Communications et al. [The Wesbecker Case]. Jefferson Circuit Court, Division, 1, Louisville, Kentucky, No. 90-CI-06033, Volume XVI, 1994.

Ferketick, A. K. et al. "Depression as An Antecedent to Heart Disease among Women and Men

252

in the NHANES I Study," National Health and Nutrition Examination Survey. *Archives of Internal Medicine* 160, no. 9 (2000): 1261–1268.

Food and Drug Administration (FDA). "FDA Statement Regarding the Anti-depressant Paxil for Pediatric Population" (June 19, 2003); on the Internet: *www.fda.gov/cder/drug/infopage/ paroxetine/default.htm.*

Frank, E. Et al. "Efficacy of Treatments for Major Depression," *Psychopharmacology Bulletin* 29 (1993): 457–475.

Gorski, Terence T. "Depression and Relapse," Professional Counselor Magazine (December 1995).

Hammond, Lisa M., and Terence T. Gorski. *Working the Program.* Independence, Missouri: Herald House Independence Press, 2005.

Lebowitz, B.D. et al. "Diagnosis and Treatment of Depression in Late Life: Consensus Statement Update," *Journal of the American Medical Association* 278 (1997): 1186–1190.

Moorside, Haddad P. "Do Antidepressants Have Any Potential to Cause Addiction?" Trafford General Hospital, Davyhulme, Manchester, UK. *J Psychopharmacol* 13, no. 3 (1999): 300–307; on the Internet: *http://www.biopsychiatry.com/ addictionp.htm.*

NIMH—National Institute of Mental Health. *Depression,* NIH Publication No. 02-3561 (2000, reprinted September 2002); on the Internet: *http://www.nimh.nih/gov/publicat/ depression.cfm.*

Preda, A. et al. "Antidepressant-associated Mania and Psychosis Resulting in Psychiatric Admission," *Journal of Clinical Psychiatry* 62 (2001): 30–33.

Robins, L. N., and D. A. Regier, eds. *Psychiatric Disorders in America, The Epidemiologic Catchment Area Study.* New York: The Free Press, 1990.

Rubinow, D. R. et al. "Estrogen-Serotonin Interactions: Implications for Affective Regulation," *Biological Psychiatry* 44, no. 9 (1998): 839–850.

Schmidt, P.J. et al. "Differential Behavioral Effects of Gonadal Steroids in Women with and in Those without Premenstrual Syndrome," *Journal of the American Medical Association* 338 (1998): 209–216.

Van Putten, T. "Why Do Schizophrenic Patients Refuse to Take Their Drugs? *Archives of General Psychiatry* 31 (1974): 67–72.

_____. "The Many Faces of Akathisia," *Comprehensive Psychiatry, International Journal of Neuropsychopharmacology* 2 (1975): 165–172.

Vitiello, B. and P. Jensen. "Medication Development and Testing in Children and Adolescents," *Archives of General Psychiatry* 54 (1997): 871–876.

Wyeth Pharmaceuticals. "Dear Health Care Professional" (August 22, 2003). Reported in "Suicidality, Violence and Mania Caused by Selective Serotonin Reuptake Inhibitors (SSRIs): A

Review and Analysis," *International Journal of Risk & Safety in Medicine* 16 (2003/2004): 31–49.